The Gods of the Hindus

The Gods of the Hindus

Om Lata Bahadur

📖 UBSPD
UBS Publishers' Distributors Ltd.
New Delhi • Bangalore • Chennai
Calcutta • Patna • Kanpur • London

UBS Publishers' Distributors Ltd.

5 Ansari Road, New Delhi-110 002
Phones: 3273601, 3266646 • Cable: ALLBOOKS • Fax: 3276593, 3274261
E-mail: ubspd@gobookshopping.com • Website: www.gobookshopping.com

10 First Main Road, Gandhi Nagar, Bangalore-560 009
Phones: 2253903, 2263901, 2263902 • Cable: ALLBOOKS
Fax: 2263904 • E-mail: ubspd.bng@bgl.vsnl.net.in

6, Sivaganga Road, Nungambakkam, Chennai-600 034
Phones: 8276355, 8270189 • Cable: UBSIPUB • Fax: 8278920
E-mail: ubspd.che@md4.vsnl.net.in

8/1-B, Chowringhee Lane, Kolkata-700 016
Phones: 2441821, 2442910, 2449473 • Cable: UBSIPUBS
Fax: 2450027 • E-mail: ubspdcal@calvsnl.net.in

5 A, Rajendra Nagar, Patna-800 016
Phones: 672856, 673973, 686170 • Cable: UBSPUB • Fax: 686169
E-mail: ubspdpat1@sancharnet.in

80, Noronha Road, Cantonment, Kanpur-208 004
Phones: 369124, 362665, 357488 • Fax: 315122
E-mail: ubsknp@sancharnet.in

Distributors for Western India:
M/s Preface Books
Unit No. 223 (2nd floor), Cama Industrial Estate,
Sun Mill Compound, Lower Parel (W), Mumbai-400 013
Phone: 022-4988054 • Telefax: 022-4988048 • E-mail: Preface@vsnl.com

Overseas Contact:
475 North Circular Road, Neasden, London NW2 7QG, UK
Tele: (020) 8450-8667 • Fax: (020) 8452 6612 Attn: UBS

© Om Lata Bahadur

First Published 2001
First Reprint 2002

Cover Design: Abhiroopa

Printed at Rajkamal Electric Press, Delhi (India)

To
My Family

Preface

I take my pen with humility and with bowed head and fold my hands to all the symbols and facets of the 'Almighty' — that I have been taught to worship and respect — who are steeped in my being from my very childhood, and in whom I find 'divinity' — both by my reason and my faith.

I am neither competent enough to go into the deeper philosophies of the ancient writings nor can I hope to do justice even to this work — yet I will try to put across as simply as I can — the concept of the Hindu Gods and Goddesses.

—Om Lata Bahadur

Acknowledgements

My greatful thanks to Mrs Anita Mathur who deligently translated the 'Artis' in English from chaste Hindi. She is a great scholar of Sanskrit and was helped by her husband Sri Harsh Kumar Mathur who is the head of the Department of Sanskrit at the 'St. Stephens College', Delhi.

My very great thanks to Miss Usha Mathur who has edited and corrected the translations of the 'Artis' into Roman and English.

Last but not least my thanks to Abhiroopa, who has made all the illustrations including the cover, for the book.

Contents

Introduction

There is a great deal of curiosity about the different gods that exist in the Hindu pantheon and how an ancient and intelligent race accepts the many different faces of various Gods whom they have worshipped for thousands of years and keep on worshipping even today. Not only in villages where there is blind faith and a good deal of superstition, but in the cities of India where the intelligentsia resides, huge temples are erected to our 'Monkey God Lord Hanuman' and the all-benevolent 'Lord Ganesh' with the face of an elephant, and also the different forms of 'devis' — like Durga with ten hands and Kali having her red tongue hanging out and looking very very ferocious. Hundreds of other gods are worshipped with great devotion by every Hindu.

I have illustrated in my book that the Hindu is neither a fool nor an illiterate person but does his worship with pure faith in the oneness of the Almighty represented in different forms. God, as the basic Hindu belief, is the duality of the mighty 'Soul'. One is the 'Supreme' — the Unmanifest — and the other living individually in each creature. The ultimate aim of the separated souls is to evolve themselves by virtue of their good 'karma' in their successive incarnations on this earth, and ultimately merge with the 'Unmanifest' — who has no face and no body and sits on no throne but is present everywhere.

In Hindu belief, God resides within you and the soul is indestructable and, therefore, a part of God: No manifestation of form is ungodly and to bring people nearer to God is to give 'Him' a shape; and as He is all shapes, He can be represented and worshipped in any form that the worshipper desires. There are thirty-three crore and thirty lakh Hindu 'deities'.

All religions have something concrete to meditate upon. They hold a shrine or idol or book so holy that to talk without respect for it is the greatest sacrilege — although it is only a symbol of the 'Unmanifest' — and the 'Unmanifest' is absolutely free and beyond reproach.

The Hindu has a very romantic religious philosophy and is free to picturise any model to worship that pleases him. Along the ages, the Aryans who coded this dharma with practice assimilated forms that were already being worshipped by the original inhabitants of 'Bharatvarsh' and gathered them in their fold, for nothing is beyond the fold of a true Hindu and he is 'bound' by no dogmas.

The Hindu believes that good and bad are both parts of Nature and must co-exist as ordained by the Almighty. Each *yug* is predestined to have one or the other as the dominant factor.

Satya Yug — age full of goodness (Duration 17,28,000 years of man): The age when goodness prevails over evil.

Treta Yug — age three parts of goodness (Duration 12,96,000 years of man): Evil starts to creep in to a limited extent only. Ram Avtar lays down the *dharma* of each individual according to his or her station in life.

Daupar Yug — equal parts of goodness and evil (Duration 8,64,000 year of man): Evil becomes more and more dominant, as more and more people inhabit the earth and jealousy and greed start showing their teeth. Krishna comes to teach the people how to overcome evil, while doing ones duty even if it involves killing of those that invite disaster. He teaches how to overcome greed and selfishness, and tide over the unhappy and turbulent period that was to be called 'Kalyug' which would follow his death.

Kalyug — three parts evil and one part good (Started on the midnight of 17th-18th February 3102 BC has a true span of 4,32,000 years of man): When evil will be the most dominant, as the world overflows with people — then the Kalki Avtar will appear and solve the problems by His warlike qualities — He will come on a white horse with a sword in his hand. Even God cannot change the nature of the 'yugs'. They have been ordained and shall remain so. Krishna left the teachings in the words of the *Bhagwat Gita* for humans to tide over the rule of evil and reach the age of truth 'Satya Yug' again.

The Hindu has only one Supreme Deity 'Ishwar' or 'Bhagwan' or 'Brahman' — The One, The Supreme, The Unmanifest, all pervading — all-powerful, Omniscient, Omnipresent and Omnipotent. He in Himself encompasses all actions — good or bad, active or still, thought is even Him. He sits on no throne and He has no form or body. He is everywhere. In all living beings the 'Supreme' resides, all creation is His and that is His Nature.

He becomes individualistic in an individual — be it animal, insect, bird or a human being. Thus the Hindu believes in the duality of the Soul, one, the 'Supreme Soul' and the other in the living body of a being. *The Bhagwat Puran* likens this to the presence of air which is unmanifest and yet is all around us in the atmosphere — but as a part of the essential breath it becomes individualistic and belongs to the being that holds it within itself. As soon as it is exhaled, it mixes again with the 'Whole' and loses its separate identity. That is the ultimate aim of the separated soul within each living being, to merge with the 'Whole'. The reason for this is again the 'nature' of the Almighty.

The Hindu believes in Reincarnation — that the being is born again and again until it reaches perfection and is without sin, then it is automatically lifted unto the Supreme Soul. He believes that there are eighty-four lakh forms an individual soul has to take to reach the highest form of a human being. It is superior to all others as it has, in addition to a superior brain, a conscience and the ability to judge right from wrong. But it can fall even after reaching this human stage if it strays from the right path of Truth — and then can fall from the ladder of the highest evolvement to anywhere down the line depending on his *karmas* (actions), and *karm* becomes the cause which determines the next birth and becomes destiny. All *karmas* of previous lives play their part in each new reincarnation, cancelling out good or bad as the case may be. But free will is mixed up with destiny like milk and water, and cannot be separated. No one knows where free will plays its part or the action is due to the previous *karmas*.

The path to salvation is three-fold. They are:

1. *Chittasany mana* — Mind is the cause of freedom of the coils of senses. Control the mind.
2. *Bhakti* (complete devotion) is a prerequisite for salvation.
3. *Knowledge* is attained by reading the scriptures written by the great rishis which are full of deep thought, philosophy and meditation.

It is said that Hinduism is a way of life, and it is true that Hinduism has no dogmas. The name Hindu was coined by the foreigners of the West who became aware that the people living across the Sindhu River (Indus) were following a way of life and belief very different from theirs — and not coming across a definite name for them, they called them Hindus synonymous with the name of the river 'Sindhu'. The actual name of what has been followed by those that lived on the other side of the river was 'Sanatan Dharma' or the 'eternal law' and it had become the 'dharam' (duty) to adhere to it. The law was as natural as Nature itself and Nature is the Will of God — following it leads automatically to a healthy, controlled and contented life. Natural laws are simple, e.g. if you jump off a cliff you are most likely to die or at least break your bones; if you are unpleasant to your fellow man, he shall be unpleasant to you. On the other hand, if you are pleasant or helpful to others they in turn will be helpful and pleasant to you. Even in daily life, if things are done systematically and honestly at the right time, life will run smoothly as intended and no sin shall be incurred. Sin is hurting others knowingly and that is what brings the human being back to face this world again and again to atone for the wrong doings. But a person leading a life of selfless devotion to 'duty' or 'dharm' breaks the cycle of rebirth and attains the state of 'moksh' (freedom) or merging with Supreme Spirit.

The philosophy was developed in the Indian sub-continent of ours — when the Aryans spread out from the grassy plateaus of Central Asia towards east and west, and one branch made its way into this sub-continent.

The Aryans were a very intelligent race, handsome, fair skinned, tall with sharp features and broad foreheads maybe decendants of people from a dying planet who had found the earth, a fit place to settle down. They were a nomadic race and on seeing the beautiful flat land of northern India with its rivers and water resources, they soon took to the plough, settled down in permanent settlements and called it 'Aryavarta', later Bharatvarsh.

They recognised that there were certain rules that had to be followed to live in a permanent social order. With their pristine wisdom and powerful brain, they formulated the rule in a system of conduct, coded them into *slokas* (stanzas) in their language Sanskrit and called them the *Vedas* — which they guarded with great care. They taught the *slokas* by word of mouth to their youngsters and when writing became known the learned men — the *rishis* — wrote them down in chaste Sanskrit and took great pains to keep the pronunciation very exact and clear so that when *slokas* recited the rhythm and clarity did not distort the words and was pleasant to the listeners.

The hymns and *slokas* and *mantras* travelled to the rest of the country through word of mouth, and their pronunciation and meaning was the same all over the country.

There is complete harmony in the ancient sound and writing of Sanskrit written thousands of years ago and the one read and written today. The chanting of Sanskrit *slokas* and *mantras* are as pure and beautiful today as they were when the Aryans came into India.

The great books containing the *slokas* are the four great and holy *Vedas* which are the most prized possession of the Hindus. They still carry the same meaning as when they were being learnt by word of mouth and repetition, and are secure in their original text in written Sanskrit.

The *Vedas* are purported to have been given to mankind by 'Brahma' Himself, the Aspect of the Almighty who created the Universe with special attention to the three worlds that the Hindu believes exist and are inhabited. These words of wisdom of the *Vedas* are on every conceivable subject which the human mind strives to know — with details of the methods — practices and usage, and how they are to be interpreted in thought and action.

These four *Vedas* contain the story of creation of human history, philosophy and conduct — rules for all occasions and the duties assigned to each individual according to his or her age, status, occupation and capability. This later gave rise to the caste system as people tended to follow the trade of their fathers and forefathers, to which they were accustomed and had learnt automatically from childhood.

The *Vedas* were compiled and written down by great *rishis* who lived in hermitages away from the realms of Kings and common men, in beautiful surroundings near the sacred rivers or on the Himalayas, and are the most revered books in the Hindu way of life. The Rig Veda was the only one during Satyug the rest were compiled later.

They four *Vedas* are:

1. *Rig Veda*
2. *Yajur Veda*
3. *Sam Veda*
4. *Atharva Veda*

Then came the *Purans* and *Upnishads* explaining the great works in such a manner as to make their hidden meaning easier for the common man and also to keep his interest and devotion intact for generations to come. Those who wrote these interwove them with stories to delight the mind of the listeners as they mixed the Celestial Being whom they created from their imagination with the human being — thus bringing the gods and demi-gods, devtas and demons on the same level as the human beings in their desires, in their love and hate and the general life pattern of marriage and birth. This made it easier for the *rishis* and the sages to keep the people on the right path as these stories contained very deep philosophy and trained the mind to think in the manner of the *Vedas* with ease and comfort. Then came the Epics which were written to illustrate the greatness of the kings and people who followed the *Vedas*. These were the *Ramayana* and the *Mahabharata*.

The Aryans did not worship any idol but performed *havans* and *yagyas* under the open skies by pouring oblations into the fire to legendary beings or the imagined Gods who had proved of extreme usefulness to the human race and so had attained the status of *devtas*. The Aryans' practice was of giving great respect to one who proved indispensable to mankind and they gave such a being the pedestal of a demi-god.

The *havans* were performed in great style and with a great deal of pomp. Many sages were present in the ones performed usually by kings and known as *yagyas*, which were usually performed for a specific purpose. Great preparations were made and became grand affair. Many are mentioned in the holy scriptures. *Havans* could even be performed by householders in a private ceremony. Sages would do them more or less everyday as a form of prayer. Pure ghee was poured as oblation along with many types of grain and seeds and sweet smelling medicinal herbs in between chanting of Vedic *mantras* and hymns. This made the atmosphere pure, clear and sweet smelling for miles around. The sonorous sound of the Vedic text filled the entire region with a sense of purity and elation and brought peace to the soul; the smoke and sweet smell reached up to heaven and the gods beseeching them to bestow upon the performer the boons he had asked for.

Then slowly the imaginative, artistic and poetical nature of the Aryans brought the Almighty nearer to mankind as they gave shape to the three Great Powers of the 'Unmanifest Ishwar'. There was no sacrilege involved in giving Him a human form with all its beauty — since all creation had a spark of divinity and a soul was one with the Supreme in its eventuality of which man was the highest in the evolution of life. The three main powers of Creation, Preservation and Destruction had been named earlier and were already being called Brahma, Vishnu and Mahesh. They were brought to earth as a three-faced human image with a single neck and torso, all facets of the same Supreme Power equal in strength and wisdom — never dying — possessing all qualities of the Almighty, but with different tasks specifically assigned to each aspect.

This enabled men to concentrate their minds on a definite form in their prayer and meditation. The mind did not have to wander in its effort to imagine the Unmanifest. This then was the beginning of the Idol and great temples were built around which the town revolved. It became a focal point for people to meet and have interaction with one another, without which normal human existence becomes impossible — so it has been ordained — the temple became the hub of great activity.

Since the three aspects had their different identities and tasks — they soon became distinct personalities in the minds and hearts of the people and who soon separated them into different 'Beings' and breathed life into them, and they became alive to intermingle with the inhabitants of the earth and the two other worlds that a Hindu believes exist along with this *Mrityu Lok* — as our world is called. The other two are *Satya Lok* (or *Dev Lok*) which houses all the devtas and also those that died with many good deeds and are given rest for sometime in heaven. The third is the *Pataal Lok* — for the ones with more evil than good in them and are known as 'asuras' and also those who have done evil deeds in this world and must return in any form their *karm* has earned for them. *Pataal Lok* also houses all the snakes.

Thus the plural form of 'Bhagwan' was created and soon enough each activity of 'Nature' took a form for the Hindus. These different facts of 'Ishwar' became very numerous as the Aryans also absorbed what the natives of India were already worshipping in different parts of the country and mingled it with one or the other aspect already accepted by them. Thereby the same aspect could have two or three faces or forms with slight variations in their duties. This enabled the natives to take easily to the Aryans' fold. These manifestations were 'demi-gods' — they were born of the Gods themselves or created by them and could bestow boons and graces to their worshippers on their own initiative, but to a limited extent laid down by the Supreme Powers which held the reins completely in its hold and had 'absolute authority'. The devtas living in *Dev Lok* also had powers to bestow but to an even lesser extent than the demi-gods.

It is like our body whose organs and parts act independently having a particular task to perform. The action seems absolutely independent and yet the command must come from the all-powerful brain, which is guided by an unseen intelligence. That is how the Hindus educated or uneducated takes these hundreds of gods (since demi-gods are also addressed as such) in their stride — the learned with wisdom and knowledge and the uneducated with faith. Not one will ridicule the worship of an idol or picture in a temple or at home of any accepted form. As in whatever you see God, He exists there.

They also believed that Lord Vishnu — the Preserver — comes down to earth in the form of any new manifestation of life taking a different form for the progress of the soul towards its evolvement in becoming 'a human being' and so is the first of a new specie and is called a new and different 'avtar'. This can easily be understood since all creatures are a part of Vishnu — any new specie is a new form of Him in a new garb and, as said before, He is known as an *avtar*. These earlier *avtars* are:

Animal Forms

1. Matsya: Fish which lives submerged in water from where life begins.
2. Kurmi *avtar*: Tortoise — the form which can live in water as well as on land.
3. Varaha *avtar*: Boar — which lives on land but can also swim.
4. Narsingh *avtar*: Lion — fierce and ready to face the world on the land itself, more or less a complete land animal. He is portrayed as half-lion and half-man.

These *avtars* are ones that work by instinct and not reason. They are known as *bhogi* and are progressing in their onward journey towards the desired goal of perfection.

When life takes the form of a human being the work of the *avtar* becomes intellectual and Vishnu takes the human form only when *adharam* takes over from *dharam*, order has to be re-established in this world and the path to righteousness and duty taught and again established — He comes as a true human being and is born, lives, suffers and enjoys as one of us but is a superior being recognisable by his action and deeds.

Human Forms

1. Vaman (Dwarf): The first of the human specie.
2. Purusram (Angry Man): Seems to have cleared up the forest for habitations and destroyed those that were aggressive.
3. Ram (Perfect Man): Who taught duty and right action to the human race.
4. Krishna: He is not an *avtar* but is accepted as 'Puran Bhagwan' (Absolute God) as He was born in the full form of Vishnu with four hands and all the symbols in them, but soon became a normal baby before the eyes of Vasudev and Deviki his parents.
   Balram: Krishna's brother was the man with great strength and worked a plough. He is supposedly the *avtar* and brings in agricultural produce to a fast growing population and food.
5. Buddha: The one with no wants or desires, teaching complete austerity.
6. Kalki: The *avtar* yet to come — to destroy evil of Kalyug — and herald the age of truth and righteousness 'Satyug'. He rides on a white horse and has a sword in his hands.

These reminiscences of the Darwin's theory of evolution in its essential sense and meaning — that each new manifestation of life is recognised as an advancement of the specie.

Life began from the sea; the main incarnations of 'Vishnu' as *avtar* in totality are:

1. Maach *avtar* (Fish)
2. Kurmi *avtar* (Tortoise)
3. Varaha *avtar* (Boar)
4. Narsingh *avtar* (Half man-half lion)

His incarnations as a Karm bhogi are:

5. Vaman (Dwarf Man)
6. Parusram (Angry Man): Who killed the aggressive Vishatriyas when they became too strong.
7. Ram (Perfect Man)
8. Krishna: Krishna gave the Bhagwat Gita' the truth about life.
9. Buddha: Teaching austerity and ahimsa.
10. Kalki: Still to come satan.

> Dharm or Hinduism is pragmatic and Catholic in its religion or 'dharam' and in its essense is no different from any other. There is no difference in man's search for 'Truth' and 'God' — and what that is — must be universally the same for all and God only knows what 'that is'!!

Any place of worship brings the best in those who have been taught to associate it with great piety, be it a building — an idol or a book or even a symbol — be it at home or in a temple or any place of prayer — it brings out the best vibrations in a person. These vibrations are absorbed by the symbol and that symbol reflects back goodness and blessing to whosoever goes to receive them with a pure and open heart and mind. That is the belief of the Hindus.

In the early stages the gods were mainly in the form of men, although the female form was also prevalent as consorts. The emphasis was on male Gods — they had full power to control their spouses who on their own had very little authority — they usually asked their husbands to bestow boons and favours and were shown to be submissive to their lord and master. There were some female deities like mother earth but no temples were created for them. They were respected as a mother — in a home, but the main patriarch was always the father. So it was with the Gods.

Much later the concept of 'Devi' as an independent Goddess was developed by the Aryans, although there was worship of a female deity by the natives of this land. It was more fright than any other thing and the Aryans absorbed her mainly in the 'Kali' aspect of the Goddesses and even in the 'Durga' aspect to some degree. Soon the Goddesses included Saraswati, Laxmi and Parvati. According to the 'Bhagwat Puran' just before *Kalyug* (of today which began about 5000 years ago) that 'Devi' became a powerful deity on her own strength and more temples were built in her honour than of the male Gods.

There is a story of how Devi descended on the earth to be worshipped:

It came about thus — Although Kans killed all the children born to Vasudev and Devki as he had been told that the eighth child would be the one that would kill him, he kept both Vasudev and Devki in prison for all the while the eighth was born — yet Krishna had an elder brother 'Balram' only a year or two older to him. Vasudev had six more wives but they had all gone into hiding. One Rohini was left at Gokul with Vasudev's friend — Nand.

Before Vishnu came as Puran Avtar in the form of Krishna, he proclaimed that the serpent Adishesh to be the 'Avtar' and wanted him to be his elder brother Balram. So when Devki conceived Balram, Vishnu called a celestial being named Yog Maya, a denizen of heaven, and told her that Adishesh who was an Ansha of Narayan 'Himself' — was in the womb of Devki and that she should go at once to Mathura and extract the child from Devki's womb and place it in the womb of Rohini at Gokul. He told her that Devki's next child will be 'HE' 'Himself' and that she will be born as the child of Yashoda and Nand at Gokul from where Vasudev will take her to Mathura in exchange for Krishna and Kans will try to kill her but she would fly out of his hand as lightening and declare: "The birth of the one who would kill Kans had been born and he was safe. Because of this great event Jog Maya would be famous for all future times, she will be known as 'Ishwari' and will be able to grant all the boons people ask for — when they pray to her. Men will worship her with incense and sacrifice. "People will build temples for you and you will be known by as many names as — Durga — Bhadrakali — Vijaya — Vaishnavi — Kumuda — Chandalika — Krishna — Kanika — Maya — Narayani — Iswari — Sharda and Amibka", so said Krishna.

Yog Maya took the permission of the Lord and descended to the earth. Devki went into a trance and the transfer of the child was performed without her knowing about it. The next day people believed that the child had been lost without being born. Kans also heard the same tale.

Yog Maya was then born as a girl child to Yashoda, with whom Vasudev exchanged Krishna on Janmasthmi night. She is the one whom Kans came to kill, but when he lifted her and wanted to throw her on the ground, she flew out of his hands saying, 'Kans, the one who is your slayer is born and is safe on this earth' and vanished as lightning. So it was that a female deity came in the world to be worshipped in many forms surpassing many of the male demi-Gods in her powers and strength and is attributed with the killing of many asuras and demons. She is ferocious as 'Kali' and benevolent as 'Durga' but in all her incarnations she carries all the attributes of 'God' and perhaps more people pray to her than to any other God or demi-Gods.

The term God is used for the Devtas Demi-gods and the 'Supreme being' and the usage is in complete harmony because each power of God leads to the 'Supreme' in any case, only the facet differs. It depends in whom the worshipper has found peace and in which particular image of the Almighty — he sees his God.

The conception of God for a Hindu — is the entirety of the Universe. He is described in the Vedas as the 'Virat Purush'. He really should be the Universal form of meditation. The description of 'The Virat Purush' as written in the Vedas.

The soles of the 'Virat Purush' form the Patal Lok (one of the seven regions below the earth).

His insteps are Rasatala and His heels are Mahatala (two of the seven region belows the earth).

His ankles are Talatala and the knees the Sutala (again two of the regions below the earth).

His thighs form Vitala and Atala (the last two of the seven regions below the earth).

Bhutala (earth) forms the back of His waist.

The sky is the naval.

The heavens or Paradise forms his chest (the fourth of the seven loks above the earth) and Jana (Gyan) is His face.

Tapolok is his forehead (the world above Janalok). Satyalok (the abode of Brahma) is the uppermost lok of the seven loks above the earth. The arms are the Devtas and the four quarters His ears. The nostrils are the Ashwani twins and fire is His mouth. The Aantariksh (the region between heaven and earth) with its Sun and Moon form His eyes.

The ocean is His stomach and the mountains form His bones.

The rivers are His veins and the hair on His body are the trees.

His stride is time and the Air is His breadth.

The clouds make up his looks and the evening His clothing.

The Auyakta (the unknown) is his heart and Chandra is His mind which is all light (Mahat).

His ego (ahankar) is Rudra and Yajna (sacrifice) is the action.

'Bhagwan' is the Purush and is the soul of the entire Universe.

Translated by Kamla Subrahmanium in the
Bhagwatam Puran

The Gita where Lord Krishna describes the Eternal Being to Arjun in its thirteenth Discourse is thus — I will declare — that which ought to be known and that which being known immortality is enjoyed — the beginingless Supreme (Eternal' called neither being nor non-being.

Everywhere that hath hands and feet every where eyes, heads, and mouths, all hearing, He dwelleth in the world enveloping all.

Shining with all sense — faculties but without any senses, unattached, supporting every thing, and free from qualities (guna) but enjoying qualities.

Without and within all beings, immovable and also moveable, by reason of His subtely imperceptible, at hand and far away is 'That'. Not divided amid beings, and yet seated distributively. That is to be known as the supporter of beings. He devours and He generates.

That the light of all lights, is said to be beyond darkness. Wisdom, the object of wisdom, by wisdom to be reached, seated in the hearts of all thus knowing enters into 'My Beings'.

Translated by Annie Besant

Brahma

Brahma

According to the oldest theory mentioned in the Rig Veda, the origin of the universe was when Brahma the creator was born out of a golden egg 'Hiranyagarbha' which came into the infinite space by the desire of the 'Supreme Cause' and after lying in it for a year He divided it into two parts, the upper part formed the heaven and the lower one formed the universe and between them was the sky or the space which is ever expanding known as Brahmand derived from the word 'brish' which means to expand. It seems that the present theory of the 'Big Bang' which was the cause of the universe was accepted by these early Aryans and they seem to know then what is now the most widely accepted theory concerning the origin of the universe. Brahma is fair and often portrayed as an old man with four faces with a white beard. He is seated on a lotus usually. His abode is *Brahm Lok.*

The most accepted theory of the common man today is that Brahma sitting on a lotus — with a long stem that is rooted in the naval of Narayan appears at the time when the desire of Narayan to create again is awakened — after the great deluge of *Maha praley* — when only 'He' remains reclining on the coiled up 'Adishesh'. The great original serpent serenely floating in the vast ocean of the universe in complete harmony with 'Himself' as all else has been withdrawn into 'Him' and there is no action.

3

The cycle must begin again and the creative power of 'Narayan' comes in the form of 'Brahma' to bring life and action in the three worlds.

Brahma is asked to create the universe again with special attention to our world. Brahma is shown as having four heads. He was even attributed with five in the earlier times. One story is that he had only one head when he came out of the naval of Narayan. To create he needed a female form also. So he created a woman named 'Satyaroopa' from his own body. She had hundred forms and hundred expressions. She was very beautiful and Brahma fell in love with his own creation and could not take his eyes off her. She felt bewildered and shy and tried to get away from his gaze. So he created three more heads to be able to see her wherever she went. Satyaroopa rose up into the sky and Brahma created one more on top of his head but this was burnt off by Shiva's third eye when Brahma once talked disparagingly of Shiva.

The other story is that when Brahma found himself alone on the lotus, he looked all around and discovered that he had four heads pointing in the four directions. He saw nothing but a large expanse of water all around him and the noise he heard was of the waves and it seemed to him that they said *"tap! tap.* Perform *tap* and you will find what you seek."* He meditated for a hundred years and was absorbed in this *tap.* All of a sudden he saw the form of 'Narayan' resting on the milk white serpent Adishesh and at once knew that he was the 'Purush' (the absolute) and also knew what was expected of him as wisdom descended on him. He worshipped his other self in the form of 'Narayan' with words of praise that came out of him without having being taught. Narayan said, "I have set you the task of creating the world and all beings". Brahma said "so be it" and got off the lotus.

Out of his mind were born the four rishis — Sanaka, Sanada, Sanatana and Sanat Kumar and he commanded them to take up the work of creation but the four refused —

they only wanted salvation and none of the problems of the world. Brahma got very angry with them but could do nothing about it. He held his anger — still it came out of his forehead as a reddish blue crying baby and this was not quite the type of people Brahma wanted to create — still on the child's pleading he was given the name 'Rudra' and told him to dwell in the hearts — in the senses — in the sky, air, fire, water, earth, in the sun and the moon wherever anger sometimes takes over control. "You are at liberty to produce beings in your own image," Brahma told Rudra. He later on became identified with Lord Shiva.

Brahma then created ten sons from his own body. These were — Atri — Angiras — Pulustya — Kratu — Bhrigu — Daksha — Marichi — Vasistha — Narad-Dharm and Adhram were also born of Brahma. His shadow became Kardam. His body and mind created the entire world. And out of his four faces were born the four Vedas.

Brahma then divided his body into two — one male and one female. The male was Swayambhoo (self-created — therefore, it was Brahma himself). Manu and the female 'Sataroopa', also known as Saraswati or Savitri, known also as Vach or Vaac (speech). And to these two were born three daughters and two sons. The daughters were Akruti, Prasuti and Devahuti. The sons were Puyavarte and Utanapada.

Akruti was married to a rishi named Ruchi, Devhuti to Kardan, Prasuti to Daksh; and the children of these descendants populated our world.

These legends are about the same as the Christian belief of Eve being created from the left side of Adam. The theory seems to have been carried by the Aryans to all parts of the world, so the story of creation in all major religions seems to come from the same source and belief.

Swayambhoo Manu asked his father where they were to live since the earth was submerged in the waters. Brahma went to seek the help of Narayan and then it was that

Narayan took the form of a 'varah' (the boar) as his third 'avtar' — went down to the bottom of the ocean and on his two tasks brought mother earth out of the depths. On the way he had to battle with an 'asur' named Hirnayaksha for a long time and then made dents in the ocean with his paws and placed the earth on top of the waters and handed the reins of administration to Vishnu — the 'Preserver' — after which Brahma had nothing much to do with the governing of his Creation, but Brahma is always there and is ever ready to grant 'boons" easily to those who pray to him with sincerity and sincere meditating, be it a human being, devta or demon. He often has to run to Vishnu for help because he has granted the boon to an evil person who creates problems for the devtas and the people of the earth by the strength of that very boon. Brahma himself cannot interfere with the administration of the three worlds as Vishnu has taken complete charge; and all problems fall into his jurisdiction.

Brahma has four hands and carries a kamandal in one hand, a rosary in the second and the four vedas in the third, while the fourth is held in the form of a Mudra, known as 'abhay' or it can also hold a bow or a spectre or even a ladle. His vahan (vehicle) is a 'goose'.

According to the Hindu mythology, time is counted by his day and night which is 4.320 million man years forming one day and the same of the night, there are 360 days and 360 nights which is one year of Brahma — hundred such years form a cycle, then *maha praley* takes place when even Brahma is absorbed by Narayan along with the entire universe. Now we are in the 51st year of Brahma.

Brahma is not worshipped anywhere else except at one temple dedicated to him (in the whole of India). This is in Pushkar in Rajasthan. The story attached to this predicament

of his is due to his not paying attention to his wife Saraswati.
It goes like this:

Once Brahma was performing a big yagna at Pushkar
(now in Rajasthan) and was waiting for his wife to come and
sit by his side, since no yagna can be performed without the
consort. Brahma was very agitated because Saraswati like
all women took time in dressing up and got very late. The
mahurat was passing away swiftly, so Brahma called Gayatri
(the highest of the Vedic mantra), embodied as a beautiful
woman, to come and be his wife and married her according
to the Vedic rites there and then. She sat down on his left.
As the *yagya* began, Saraswati arrived and was so incensed
that she cursed Brahma right there saying that "from now
on no one will worship you in the three worlds except at
'Pushkar' and you will lose your glitter as a God in the eyes
of the men and devtas, although you may be the first
amongst the 'Holy Trinity'!!" Brahma tried to placate her but
she could not and would not modify the curse. So it has come
about that Brahma is only worshipped at Pushkar and has
the only temple dedicated to him built there and nowhere
else in the whole country. There are no hymns or slokas in
his praise. Slowly he lost his importance also and Vishnu and
Shiva gained all the acclaim. Maybe, humanity didn't quite
approve of being created in the first place in such a world
as this and eventually decided to ignore the one who has
landed them in such a plight and chose to pray to the
'Preserver' and the 'Destroyer' to lighten their burden on this
earth.

The Preserver Vishnu became very important and
became synonymous with the 'Almighty Bhagwan' in the
minds of the Hindus, although the three aspects are
absolutely on par with each other.

One thing is that Brahma creates and never destroys. He
is also very liberal with granting boons and is easily pleased
when prayed to without any thought as to who is praying

and asking him for a boon! He later may regret having done so because the 'asurs' became powerful when granted their boons and then he has to run to Vishnu for help, because of his reckless generosity there is chaos and disruption in the world.

Shiva also shows this generosity and it is very often because of these doings that Vishnu has to take an 'avtar' to save the three worlds. Hiranakashyap — Hiranakashap and Ravan developed their demonic powers on the strength of the boons received by them from Brahma or Shiva and eventually they fled to seek the help of Vishnu to save the world from the disastrous boons which they had given without thinking as to who these people were! For Hirangaksha — Vishnu took the Vara avtar. For Hirnakashyap — Vishnu took Narsingh avtar. For Ravan — Vishnu took Ram avtar.

Brahma should not be mixed up with Brahman. The latter is another name for the 'Unmanifest Almighty' but Brahma is the name given to the 1st aspects of that Unmanifest when it manifests itself to create life.

Brahma went into the stem of the lotus that had come out of the naval of 'Vishnu' to discover from where He had come, but could not find an end to the stem, returned without the knowledge of His real origin. When Brahma could not find out how can we humans do so!!

Vishnu

Vishnu

ord Vishnu, although one of the 'Holy Trinity' of which each is equal to the other, holds the highest status amongst the three, due to the nature of His function (of preservation and sustenance of the world). He is the most adored and exalted deity in 'Sanatan Dharam' as of today and believed to be the 'Lord Supreme' Himself. The name Vishnu is taken from the word 'Vish' which means to spread in all directions and therefore he comprises the entire Universe which is ever expanding. This conception of the expanding universe seems to be known to the early 'Aryans' as it has been mentioned before as Brahma's name is also attributed to the word 'Bish' or 'Vish', as both Brahma and Vishnu represent the same aspect.

Lord Vishnu is called 'Narayan' meaning the one who dwells in water. Nara means water and ayan is the place of dwelling. Life is supposed to have come out of water and to sustain it water is an absolute necessity. Therefore Narayan is an absolute necessity as the main one of the Holy Trinity.

He is the one that must take form when adharm 'plays havoc with creation' especially for the human race or the devtas, and then He appears in the midst of creation in any form suitable to the purpose of that time, to bring back humanity to the path of dharm or duty. The Almighty is supposed to have sixteen 'Kalas' and Vishnu can come with as many as required for that particular period. The Supreme Soul does not descend on earth but a part complete in itself descends on earth (just like a vessel of water taken from the ocean is complete in itself and yet does not diminish the vastness or the power of the sea).

Vishnu has no children of his own as all creation is his child. The other two Gods of the Trinity have children born of them and called their sons and daughters but Vishnu and his consort Laxmi look after all living beings and have enough to do without having any offsprings of their own. Vishnu is also particular in granting boon and has never given a boon to an *asur* (the evil one) while Brahma and Shiva are very liberal in bestowing them to all and sundry who pleases them, without much thought to the consequences and consequently get even themselves into trouble. As mentioned before they have to run up to Lord Vishnu for succour. In fact, all Vishnu's incarnations are indirectly due to the doings of Brahma and Shiva. Praise and hymns addressed to Lord Vishnu are in plenty in the Hindu scriptures. He is deeply loved in all his incarnations on earth as He comes face to face with humanity itself. The 'Bhagwat Puran' mentions twenty-two or even 39 avtars, but the accepted ones are ten as written already in a previous chapter.

Vishnu is portrayed as dark in colour, or one can easily say blueish, red or yellow in his incarnations during the various yugs. He is usually depicted as sleeping over the waves of the ocean reclining on the coils of the 'Sheshnag' or standing on the waves of the ocean. He is usually shown with four hands, each holding his four chief attributes. The conch shell — the discus (Sudarshan chakra), the gada (mace) and the lotus. He is shown as wearing a yellow robe tied like a beautiful *dhoti* on the lower limbs and a *aang vastra* thrown round his neck with both ends falling straight down his body. Another yellow scarf acts as a belt holding the *dhoti* at the waist. The *dhoti* is tied in a way that if forms a long flair coming down in front of both the legs. He wears a vayjanti mala (necklace) with pearls, rubies, emeralds, sapphire and diamonds, and he wears the large beautiful diamond known as 'Kaustube' which had come out of the ocean when it was churned. The conch is named 'Panchjanya' (beautiful to look at). The 'lotus' the original flower. The gada (mace or club) is named 'Kumud'. He wears a lot of other jewellery as armlets and necklaces. A crown made of gold and earrings in the shape of a crocodile known as 'Makerakati Kundal'. Across his chest is the holy thread called 'Yagyapaveela'. He also has a bow named 'Skarnga'.

In the Upnishads Vishnu Himself described the meaning of the symbols which he holds in his hands. He says that He holds the conch in one of the lower hands as a symbol of creative energy, the discus in one of the upper hands is the symbol of the mind representing dispension and liberation. The lotus in the right lower hand represents maya (illusion) that envelopes the world. In the lower left hand is the mace which devotes strength and is also a symbol of ancient knowledge. But sometimes Vishnu is depicted with only two hands — the right held up with the 'Sudarshan chakar' the destroyer of evil, and in the left hand held down is the 'conch'.

Vishnu's consort is Laxmi, the Goddess of wealth and beauty, and she opens the gate to all resources that are required by Vishnu to run the universe. She became His consort as she chose Him and came straight to his side as soon as she came out of the Ocean when it was churned. But then Vishnu is also attributed as being the husband of Bhoo-devi (mother earth) and even in some scriptures even Saraswati and Ganga are mentioned as his wives. This actually points to the 'Oneness of Brahma and Vishnu'.

Vishnu led a very colourful life while mingling with the devtas and humans. When the churning of the Ocean was taking place and the asurs were to be denied the 'amrit', He took the form of a beautiful woman named Mohini lured the asurs and made them wait while the devtas were quickly given the amrit. Of course one asur named Rahu sensed the deception and was served the amrit as he went and sat between the Sun and the Moon. They pointed him out to Vishnu who cut him in two with His discus but he had taken a few drops of the amrit already and become immortal and thus became two — Rahu and Ketu who now come and trouble the sun and the moon and eclipse them every year.

Then once when Narad munni became arrogant due to his being so near to Narayan, Vishnu created an imaginary Kingdom in which the most beautiful daugther of the king was having her 'Swaymver'. Narad fell in love with the princess as soon as he saw her and asked Vishnu to gave him his 'roop' (face figure) and Vishnu gave him a monkey's face and the poor chap became the laughing stock of the entire gathering. Vishnu at his handsome best was chosen by the Princess. This annoyed Narad no end until Vishnu explained everything to him and told him that as Vishnu had many faces as there are species on the earth he had not cheated him. He also told him not to be arrogant as He loved everyone the same and no one was dearer to Him than the other.

Once Vishnu's consort Laxmi left Him in anger and went to her father 'the ocean' and He became very poor and distraught and moved heaven and earth to get her back. The story is told in the chapter on Laxmi.

There is much to tell about Vishnu as He came to this earth as different avtars and a little is told in the chapters of the main human avtars that have been written in this book, the rest is in the vast store house of scriptures that the Hindu 'system of life' holds.

Shiva

Shiva

Shiva is the most difficult of the 'Holy Trinity' to describe. His character is the most complex amongst the three aspects of the 'Unmanifest Supreme Lord'. He is at once merciful and dreadful — most benevolent and most ruthless when angry. He is attired in just a tiger skin with snakes round his neck and arms — a necklace of human skulls and another of his favourite bead Rudraksha — His body is covered with ash. His hair is in matted strands and hang down to his chest — but also has it piled up on top of his head in a 'jatta' on which rests the moon (on the left side). The sacred river Ganga falls on his head from the heavens and then flows down to the earth. He visits the cremation grounds and has ghosts and spirits as his entourage. He dances the 'Tandav' when angry — a dance that can destroy the entire world and even the Universe. His third eye in the middle of the eyebrows can burn anything and anyone — when opened in anger. This angry aspect is named 'rudra' synonymous with the name of the child that came out of the forehead of Brahma when he was very annoyed with the four rishis — Sanskra, Sanayatak, Sankada and Sanat Kumar for not appearing to populate the world. This aspect is awesome but being a part of the 'Unmanifest Supreme Lord' He cannot be divorced from the benevolence of 'Ishwar'. The real meaning of 'Rudra' is to relieve from sorrows. Perhaps death is a release from all sorrows of life and living, hence the name.

The Aryan mind did create the destroyer in the form of Shiva, but they could not take away the Godliness from him, otherwise he would be wholly evil — which no aspect of the Almighty can be — as the paramount nature of God is merciful and loving and yet in the nature of things what has been created must have an end and that is also the doing of the Almighty. That aspect due to the fright of death and destruction — was given the garb of an austere, frightening and ill-kept God.

Yet in the true Hindu belief, creation and destruction are a continuous cycle, and death is not the end as it opens the door to another life which could and should be for the betterment of the 'Being' — depending on his or her 'karma' — so the work of Shiva as destroyer is a natural course of events in the existence of every created being or thing. And death is as natural as birth and creation. Therefore, the nature of Godliness in Shiva does not differ from that of Brahma or Vishnu.

In fact, Shiva is portrayed as being really 'naive' and is called 'Bholenath'. He is the one that circle around the world on his vehicle 'Nandi' the bull, alongwith Parvati, his consort, to see if all is well down here and if at that time a person asks for a boon it will be granted, but the wish should be right in the heart of the person at that very moment, when Shiva and Parvati are passing the spot where he or she is. Shiva and Parvati do not have a fixed time for each place, so a person must devote himself absolutely to that wish for the entire twenty-four hours. It can, of course, just happen by a coincidence that Shiva and Parvati are just there when a wish is being expressed and the wish does come true however unimaginable it could be! Does that not happen once in a while!!

Since Shiva has much to do with this world, He is equally worshipped by the Hindus of all sects and temples to Him and his consorts are as numerous as the ones to Vishnu and Laxmi.

The idea of Shiva being equal to the Creator is accepted by the Hindus even as the creative form of the Unmanifest, as his accepted form is the 'ling' depicting the pallus of the male form and the 'yoni' of the female form, in openly accepting the symbol of creation. Most temples represent Shiva in this form only. The Hindu did not fight shy of the act for creation (as given to the living beings) in his acceptance of the entirety of functions as ordained by nature.

Then Shiva is equated with Vishnu in his great interest in the three worlds and their working, when he is in his benevolent form becomes to help anyone who is devoted to him and prays to him. We have Hindus absolutely devoted to Vishnu, and others absolutely devoted to Shiva or Shankar or Mahesh as he is also called. There are strong feelings for Vishnu in the Vaishnavites and the same goes for those that follow Shiva. They wear distinctive markings on their foreheads if they are staunch followers of one or the other sect. Shiva actually means 'good', because to destroy is to recreate and Shiva regenerates. Deaths stand in the gateway of life.

The first primeval sound, the holy and eternal 'OM or 'AUM' represents Shiva as the 'Omnipresent' with all the qualities of the 'Supreme' in tact, thus accepting the three aspects to be really 'One' in its deepest meaning and is known as 'Onkar' or as 'Omkar', the one who created AUM or the first sound of the Universe.

Mahadev, as Shiva is also called, is the master and protector of the animal world also and is known as Pashupati. In this garb He controls and tames the wild animals. This is represented by Shiva wearing a tiger skin and having live snakes round his neck. He even appears in more of an animal form in some temples on the Himalayas where he is thus portrayed beside the 'ling'. The idols of the shrines of Kedarnath and Pashupati temple of Kathmandu in Nepal are testimonies to it. Shiva is also the master of the arts in the form of 'Natraj', the king of dance. The 'Tandav' is depicted as the dance of destruction which Shiva performed in grief and anger when he lost his first wife Sati and carried her body on his person and is livid with rage and melancholy. He dances in a frenzy, which nearly destroys the three worlds. The devtas had to rush to 'Vishnu' to save the world from Shiva's wrath. Vishnu summons his 'Sudarshan Chakra' and cut up the body of Sati even while it was in Shiva's hands and it fell in pieces from the grasp of Shiva who had refused to give it up and thus Vishnu succeeded in pacifying Shiva.

Another form of his dance is in peace and harmony; it is very beautiful. He dances this with his second wife Uma or Parvati (who is a reincarnation of Sati). Together they dance as one and the dance is known as 'lasya' where Shiva and Parvati become one in a form of half male and half female known as Aradha Nareeshivas. The concept of the male and female being complementary to each other and only then being complete (an equality of the sexes is accepted by the Hindus) Shiva as the male is the right side and Parvati as the female is the left side, they then complete the full human body. This depiction of Shiva is known as 'Sada Shiv' or the auspicious God in the form which has always been and shall always be — the giver of well-being, happiness and health. He is affectionately also called 'Shambhu'. In this mood He is easily pleased with little effort and fulfils wishes instantly and He is called 'Ashutosh', being generous to a fault he lands himself into difficulties and causes great anxiety to the other demi-Gods.

There is one story of a demon named "Bhasmasur" who performed Shiva's worship with singular devotion and pleased him into granting him a boon that could burn anyone on whom he placed his hand. On receiving this boon, Bhasmasur ran towards his benefactor to place his hand on Shiva himself. Shiva has to run to Lord Vishnu for help. Realising the grave situation Vishnu turned himself into a beautiful maiden and fascinated Bhasmasur by her beautiful dance. The demon forgot about Shiva and started to copy the beautiful movements of the bewitching enchantress and soon enough without knowing he put his hand over his own head in copying the dance movements of the damsel and burnt himself to death.

Shiva does not distinguish between demons and saints and any one with great 'bhakti' for him can reach him easily. Therefore he is the God of thieves, murderers, ghosts and the lesser beings even they can please him by the path of 'Bhagti'. He even created a dreadful being known as Veerabhadra who played havoc with his own father-in-law at Daksh's yagya when Sati (Shiva's first wife) threw herself in the yagna fire, because her father insulted her husband, by not inviting him for the yagna and also for not taking out a portion of the sacrifice for Him, which is a must for all Gods during a 'yagya'.

Shiva has four hands and he carries the 'Trishul' (a three-pronged trident) in the left upper hand, a damru (drum) in the right upper hand and a kamandal (a wooden bowl with a handle) in the third, the lower right is held up right in a gesture of a blessing. His neck is blue as he had drunk up the poison which had come out of the ocean when it was churned at the time of creation. He managed to confine the poison in his neck which turned blue. He sits on a tiger skin and has his consort Parvati very close to him. He lives on top of Mount Kailash in the Himalayas and travels on a white bull called 'Nandi'.

Shiva with the unkempt uncouth looks, with ash smeared all over his body, with snakes coiled round his neck, arms and 'Jatta', with the tiger skin round his waist — visiting cremation grounds and mixing with spirits and ghosts still is accepted by the mighty and holy river Ganga to fall first on his 'Jatta', because of the fear of going down straight to *Pataal Lok* due to the great force of her descent from the heavens. The benign moon accepted the 'Jatta' of Shiva as his abode as it came out of the ocean at the time of being churned by the Gods and the asurs. Parvati sits with her body senuously touching his body — yet Shiva, is untouched with either the foul or the glorious and is totally at peace within himself.

He is the only God that has children of his own. The other two aspects of the 'Supreme' Brahma and Vishnu have consorts but they have no children born of them in the manner of the living beings on the earth. Shiva and Parvati have two sons Kartik and Ganesh. Lord Hanuman is also portrayed as Shiva's son born of Anjani, the wife of Pawan — the God of the air and wind. Kartik is supposed to have been born of six different mothers from the seed of Shiva, the six of them gave birth to six different parts and then threw them in the Ganga — but the Ganga could not bear that load and instead threw them in a forest where they assembled into one known as 'Shadanan' because he had six faces — since he had six mothers. He was looked after by a divine woman named Kritikas and therefore got the name of Kartikeya. Shiva and Parvati on hearing of the birth of the son of Shiva brought him to Mount Kailash. Ganesh is also said to have been born in the absence of Lord Shiva and was said to have been born out of the scruf of Parvati's body. Both of them are accepted as Shiva's and Parvati's children, whatever the circumstances of their birth. This is the pragmatism of the Hindu religion.

Shiva is fond of *Bhung* and so his followers partake it as prasad. His worship is done by offering *behl* leaves, *bhung, dhatura, aak* and flower and fruits. *Dhatura* is poisonous and is not eaten by the worshipper but the rest is consumed by the bhakts. He is also very amorous and cannot resist a beautiful woman. Normal for the gods is what is normal for human beings in the imagination of the Hindu.

Amongst the 'asurs' Ravan and Banasur were given great favours by Shiva due to their great devotion to him. Vishnu as Ram had to come to the world to destroy Ravan and Krishna had to come to fight Banasur to whose aid Shiva came. It was a great fight and went on and on. The demi Gods and devtas had to come to the rescue of the world, which was in danger of being destroyed. Both who fought were aspects of the Supreme, Shiva on the side of Banasur and Vishnu in the form of Krishna were equal to each other, and none could win from the other. The devtas and demi Gods found a way out of the impasse and we still have the world intact for good or bad God only knows!!

Saraswati

Saraswati

Saraswati, the consort of Brahma, is the Goddess of purity — knowledge — fine arts — music and is temperamentally calm, reliable and soft. She is the one that gave language to the human race. Therefore, she is also known as Vac or Vach (meaning word). The language of the Aryans' Sanskrit both spoken and written is attributed to her.

She is portrayed as a fair-skinned, very beautiful woman dressed always in white with ornaments of gold and pearls, sitting on a lotus. She has four hands but is sometimes also shown with only two. The main hands are always playing the veena, and the third holds the counting beads of prayer — a mala of rudraksh — or even a kamandal. The fourth one has the four 'Vedas', the symbol of the greatest knowledge anyone can attain. As she is the Power of Brahma, she is the one who gave the knowledge of these holy body to Brahma himself who is also always shown as holding the 'Vedas'.

It seems that there was a great and ancient river which flowed in the plains of this sub-continent when the Aryans made their way from Central Asia across the Hindu Kush mountains and landed in the flat fertile land of this sub-continent. They came into the region of Punjab — the land of the five rivers of today. Saraswati seems to have been a very large and placid river with calm and very tasty water, which also had curative properties. Some historians believe that this river flowed from south to west and was more in Rajasthan and Punjab before it joined the Arabian Sea. But now, the most accepted theory points to its source being in the Himalayas near Badri Nath where Vyasji wrote the 'Mahabharat' and the 'Bhagwat Puran' during the Daupar Yug just before 'Kal Yug', and it seems that it is about that time that Saraswati vanished as a river due to some great upheaval. In the Bhagwat Puran, Ved Vyas seems to have got angry with her for making too much noise in her happiness on hearing that Vyasji was going to write the 'Bhagwat Puran'. The noise disturbed Vyasji's concentration and he just ordered her to vanish. She went underground. Anyway Saraswati was then supposed to have again appeared and joined the Ganga and Jamuna at Allahabad where the holy 'Sangam' is still recognised — people believe they can still see the golden waters of Saraswati coming out and joining the Ganga and Jamuna and the three in their Sangam are known as Triveni.

Some historians and researchers believe that the upheaval broke the smooth passage of Saraswati and several large ponds, lakes and streams came up at different places whatever the underground river could find an opening on the surface of the earth. Both Punjab and Rajasthan claim such reservoirs of water which are held as extremely holy and bathing in it takes one straight to heaven. Great 'Nahans' are held on auspicious days even today when millions take their bath at Kurukshetra, Pushkar and other places.

One doesn't really know where this ancient river flowed, but it was the biggest river of the time when the Aryans came into the land which they called 'Aryavarta'. It was for the first time that they found a place with plenty of fruits, herbs and eatable roots growing around the banks of the mighty river. It was a most inviting place for the Aryans to settle down and leave their nomadic life-style.

On settling down they found that they could use their vast intellect to code an harmonious co-existence between man and nature instead of perpetually running in search of food and shelter. They built permanent hamlets and cities on the banks of Saraswati which to them became a 'Goddess' in the style of their philosophy and since it gave them life and sustenance, they thought of her equal to the Creator and soon she became the 'Power of the Creator' and Saraswati — the river became synonymous with the consort of Brahma and this river whose waters they believed gave them the power to think deeply as they conjured up the wisdom of the Vedas on its banks. The two could not be differentiated and both were given the name Saraswati; which was named first is not known and in the romanticism of the Hindu thought it does not matter. Saraswati, the Goddess of wisdom, was embodied as a most beautiful woman in white with all the purity that could be bestowed on a perfect woman.

The sites of Mohanjadaro and Harappa, which seem to be two of the earliest Aryan settlements, seem to have been on the banks of Saraswati according to some researcher, but they could very well be on the banks of the 'Sindhu' which was equally huge but did not have the same curative properties. Since there is no account in the Vedas as to its location, one can only go alongwith one or the other theory of those that are doing research. One thing is certain that such a river existed before the Ganga was brought down from the high Himalayas, down to the plains of northern India by the efforts of Daleep — the father of Bhagirath — who spent a life-time in the Himalayas in his efforts to find the easiest way and method to bring this river down to 'Aryavarta' through the huge valleys and mountains of the Himalayan range. It was left to his son to eventually bring it physically to flow in a stretch of land where only the Jamuna flowed, as Saraswati seems to have vanished by that time. Jamuna, and Ganga, the twin rivers, made that area one of the most fertile and safe for the coming generations and it has been difficult for the inhabitants of 'Bharat' to find a better location for governing the subcontinent, as it slowly became one country.

Ganga took over from Saraswati the glory attributed to
a river which gave life to its inhabitants and was also
accepted as a Goddess, but the glory of Saraswati can never
be forgotten since it reached the status of Brahmas'
consort.

The stories interwoven in bringing home the truth of the
teachings of the Vedas differ sometimes in different Puranas
as they were compiled by different sages and rishis. They
are all accepted by the Hindus in his pragmatic attitude
towards these stories which he understands are really to
illustrate the right act against wrong actions and the result
thereof, especially for the uneducated and the children.
Those who having been brought up with these stories have
a natural desire to go deeper into the true philosophy of
Hinduism, and each one finds a meaning to quench his
thirst — according to the limit of his understanding, and as
the philosophy gets deeper and deeper, the understanding
also gets deeper and deeper — that is how Hinduism has
not lost its essential spiritualism and depth. Both the educated
and uneducated accept the stories and mythology in their
stride. One with intellect and the others as lessons from what
they consider actual authentic doings of the Gods and whom
they accept as the form of the 'Unmanifest', without question.

I shall tell you a story where Saraswati, Ganga and
Laxmi are all really wives of Vishnu. Ganga and Saraswati
were jealous of Laxmi who has been pampered by Vishnu.
Laxmi decided to pacify them, but they both got very angry
with her. Lord Vishnu got very annoyed at Laxmi's efforts
having been spurned and he just told Saraswati and Ganga
that henceforth he will accept only Laxmi as his Consort and
the other two will have to go down to 'Mrityu Lok' as rivers.
Ganga in the meantime cursed Laxmi to become a tree in
Mrityu Lok and so she became the 'tulsi tree' which is the
most revered in a Hindu household as it is very dear to Lord
Vishnu. Tulsi has the most amount of medicine value and by
this story the sages assured that each household would keep
a 'tulsi plant'.

Lord Vishnu of course told both Ganga and Saraswati, after He had cooled down that they will be sacred rivers and will remain near His heart always. Therefore, the Hindus without question thinks it the gateway to heaven if he takes a dip in the holy waters of Ganga and the ponds and lakes that 'Saraswati' is supposed to have become, because it is true that the waters of Ganga never get putrid or have any sort of impurity even if kept for years. It is as sparkling as it was when taken from the river especially near Haridwar and above. The waters of Saraswati also seem to possess such property which no other river in the world can boast of. It is believed that perhaps they flow over a field of radium during their journey through the mountains and no bacteria can survive in the waters — Ganga as a river and Saraswati as ponds and lakes still retain that quality.

Saraswati as a Goddess is usually shown alone, and seldom shown with Brahma in pictures and sculptures. She is a Goddess worshipped in temples or shrines because her true place is in the heart and mind, but pictures and sculputres are seen in homes — especially those that prize knowledge more than any material benefits, and it is often said that Laxmi does not reside alongwith Saraswati as they do not get along. But usually in any picture of Laxmi, one will find a small image of Saraswati, because man although extremely fond of wealth would not like to be known as a man without knowledge and therefore would not like to ignore either of them.

Saraswati's vehicle is a white long necked Swan. She is shown either on a lotus or sitting on the back of a white swan. She is also known as Savitri and Brahmani, Shatroopa and even Gayatri although in one story she is a 'sautun' of Gayatri when Brahma makes Gayatri sit beside him during a *havan* because Saraswati got late in coming!!

Saraswati puja is done on Basant Panchmi when the yellow *Sarso* greets the oncoming summer months as it is about that time she was created by Brahma. This puja is done as is usual with roli, Aapan and rice and the prasad that is offered is clarified butter, curd, honey — til, milk and ladoos. The juice of sugarcane and coconut, plums and bananas are also offered as prasad.

When a child goes to school for the first time, the name of Saraswati alongwith Ganesh is evoked and the child is asked to pray to the goddess to give him great knowledge, understanding and wisdom.

Laxmi

Laxmi

axmi, the Consort of Narain, is the most sought after
Goddess of the Hindu pantheon. She is riches
personified — and is therefore the right Consort for the
Preserver of the universe — Vishnu. She is his power of
action and the owner of all the riches that Vishnu needs —
to look after the 'world'. No one can be rich and consequently
powerful without her benevolence not even Narayan.

Laxmi came out of the ocean when at the beginning of
'time' the vast Ocean was churned to get the 'nectar' hidden
in its depths out for the benefit of the 'devtas', who wanted
to become immortal, because the 'asurs' who were stronger
to them in physique and strength were ever after their blood.
Although they were 'devtas' they were still afraid of them —
so they went to Lord Narayan to seek his help. Lord Narayan
advised them to find the amrit (nectar) from the sea and drink
it — then no one would be able to destroy them and they
would become immortal. The asurs heard about it and
demanded a share of the 'amrit'; thus it came about that both
the devtas and asurs decided to churn the ocean together
and share the nectar. Narayan quietly promised the devtas
that he would himself play such a trick that the 'devtas'
would get the entire benefit of the 'amrit' and the asurs would
get nothing at the time of distribution.

Many valuable gifts the ocean gave to the asurs. Then
all of a sudden like a streak of lightning appeared a most
beautiful and gracious woman sitting on a lotus, carrying a
garland of the same flower. Everyone stopped working as

they were bewitched by so much beauty. Everyone wanted
her, but she was the one to choose a husband for herself as
women in those days were the ones who selected their life
partners and were given full freedom in their choice.
Everyone tried to please her with beautiful gifts and great
praise in an effort to entice her, but she found some fault or
the other in all until she saw Narayan — calm and serene
and without passion that seem to affect all others. Laxmi
walked straight to him and put the garland round his neck
and stood by his side but the Lord placed her on His chest
and they both glowed like lightning in a thunder storm. After
that He could do nothing without her.

There is a story about the plight of Narayan without her
at 'Tirupati temple' at 'Tirumalai' in Tamil Nadu in the south
of India. Narayan to this day is asking his devotees to give
Him wealth and in exchange He will fulfill any and every
desire of the devotees — the more he gives the more he will
receive from the Lord, and very quickly at that, because the
Lord is in great debt!!

All this came about because once the great 'rishis'
decided on performing a great *yagya* and at the end of it
Rishi Brigu was given the task of finding out who amongst
the three great Gods — Brahma, Vishnu and Mahesh — was
fit to receive the first offering. At the end of the *yagya*, Brigu
took the offering to 'Brahm Lok' in search of Brahma, but
found him engrossed with his wife Saraswati and they did
not even hear him come! This annoyed the rishi and he
proceeded to Kailash in search of Shiva. He too was busy
making love to his wife Parvati and paid no heed to Rishi
Brigu. Containing his anger he thought he will still try out
Vishnu and went straight to Vaikunt, the abode of Vishnu and
Laxmi. They also seemed to be oblivious to everything
except themselves. The rishi turned to go in great anger at
the disrespect shown to a learned man by even 'Vishnu and
Laxmi, but at that moment Vishnu saw him and caught hold
of his feet. Brigu was so incensed that he kicked Vishnu on

his chest, still the God did not let go off his hold and appealed for forgiveness since even 'Gods' cannot show disrespect to the great amongst the mortals. This annoyed Laxmi who told Narayan in no uncertain terms that he had no business to plead with a person who had kicked her dwelling place — 'the heart of the Lord'! — but Narayan kept on asking for forgiveness from Brigu. So Laxmi left Vishnu and Vaikunt Lok and returned to her father — 'the ocean'.

Vishnu suddenly lost all his glory and riches and became very poor and powerless to do anything anymore. He loved Laxmi very much. So he made his way somehow to the ocean to find his wife and bring her back.

The Lord of the Ocean refused to part with his daughter and return her to one who had scant regard for her. For a long time he did not choose to hear the pleading of the distraught husband but finding that even his daughter was really very fond of the Lord and didn't really want to forsake him — he relented but on the condition that Vishnu would give him riches beyond human imagination and dreams — before he could take her again. The poor Lord didn't know where to get the money that his father-in-law demanded. Without Laxmi he was penniless. He thought hard and suddenly thought of Kuber — Ravan's half-brother — who had so much wealth that no one could fathom. He at once went to Kuber. After listening to Narayan's tale of woe Kuber agreed to loan him the money on a very heavy interest, which had to be paid back before the cycle of time — before *pralay* vanquished everyone and everything. The Lord promised that He will do so.

That is how Narayan made his abode at Tirupati and made it the centre of collection of funds from the human race. All and sundry would get their wishes fulfilled in return for funds, the more one gives, the more quickly his desire will be fulfilled.

Now in Kalyug the last quarter of time he still owes Kuber the interest on the loan and therefore he is in a hurry to get over with his commitment. Of course Laxmi is now with Him. Therefore, there is no dearth of money flowing into the hundies of Tirupati, but the amount of interest is huge and no one knows exactly what remains to be given still. Therefore, those who go to Tirupati temple in the town of Tirumalai and give generously, are also rewarded generously. Even prized possessions are accepted if they injure no one. Therefore people have their hair shaved as offering since one of the most prized and beautiful possession of a human being is his or her hair; except for the looks it does not harm the person as it grows again. Tirupati is the most worshipped shrine in India today and Lord Vishnu is the richest deity of the world because the amount received by the 'hundies' (a large cloth bag with its opening high but absolutely open). People put lakhs and crores in it quietly, and no one is the wiser as to who has put what in it! At the end of the day the temple trustees count up the takings and with it are run big hospitals, universities and schools and other charitable institutions for the benefit of the inhabitants of the human race. Of course Vishnu receives it and is happy for it is being used for the benefit of the people of whom he is in charge and for whom in any case he has to provide all the facilities required.

Sri is another name for riches and another name for Laxmi. She on her own can bestow riches but cannot remain at one place for long, because of a curse of Ganga and Saraswati and so is also known as Rama — one who is always on the move and fickle by nature. She is also known as *Chanchal* and no one can be ever sure when she will decide to leave. She has no qualms about how she comes and she often comes through dubious means or from the back door, therefore, her route can be through gutters and filthy paths. That is why during Diwali — the day of Laxmi puja — lighted *diyas* are a must near drains, dustbins and back entrance. Gamblers and thieves can get rich by wrongful means. But Laxmi does not remain until good is done by the people who have her and who must benefit other people.

Laxmi has become one of the most worshipped 'deity' by the Hindus as wealth and beauty are the most desired by the people, although Ganesh has to be worshipped first, a picture or idol of Laxmi will always be in every household even if Narayan is not there. On Diwali it is 'Ganesh, Laxmi' that are the paramount deities of the day. Ganesh — because no worship can take place without first worshipping him and Laxmi because it is Her day (night).

Laxmi is a docile and obedient wife and seldom gets annoyed with her husband but has been known to curse him now and then. Laxmi accompanies her spouse in his 'avtars' and was Sita with Ram and Radha (some prefer Satyabhama, since Radha was not Krishna's wife) with Krishna in the most well-known 'avtars' of Narayan.

She is shown sitting or standing on a 'lotus' when by herself and has four hands — one holding the open lotus — the other may hold a golden pitcher with mango leaves and a coconut on top of it. The third and fourth, both pointing down, have gold coins falling continuously from them. When shown with Narayan she is shown with only two hands. In some images she is supported by Narayan with his left arm around her waist while she has her right arm round his shoulder. She is also shown with Narayan reclining on 'Adishesh' floating on the eternal waters after the dissolution of the world. Laxmi and Vishnu are also shown as one and their combined image called Laxmi Narayan emphasising that they are one and cannot be separated.

Laxmi is called by various names in the Hindu scriptures, she is Shree — meaning glory and Indira because she was very pleased with Inder, the chief of the devtas, singing her praise. Kamla and Padama as she came out of the ocean sitting on a lotus carrying also a lotus garland. Lok Mata because she is the one who gives riches for the humans to be able to live. Haripriya, the beloved of Hari (Vishnu).

Although Vishnu's abode is Vaikunt, he is most often floating on the ocean bed reclining on the serpent 'Adishesh'. The name Narayan means one who resides in water and since Laxmi is the daughter of the ocean Vishnu became *Ghar Jamai* and if he can be one, so can a human being. No stigma is attached to Him on this account in the view of the Hindu thought and its scriptures.

Laxmi is the chosen deity of the Vaisyas or the trader class and every shop or trading place or a home of a Vaisya is never without a picture of Laxmi along with Ganesh.

All Hindus worship Laxmi as, without her, one is helpless. Diwali is the most lavish festival of the Hindus. It is celebrated day and night when Laxmi is worshipped with great joy and gusto. Houses are white-washed and cleaned thoroughly. Lamps are lighted and the houses decorated with shining and beautiful things. Everyone is dressed in shining and clean clothes, and jewels, gold chains in the necks, arms and ears of the women of the house since Laxmi loves glitter and loves to be amongst people of prosperity and riches. They have to be very careful with her, and not let her slip out of their hands. She can come through ways of adharm and can leave by that way also, therefore, gamble with care (Gambling is more or less a must during Diwali) for the jingle of coins delights Laxmi — but remember she is Rama and *Chanchal* and is quick to leave. Her vehicle is the owl.

Sati or Shakti

Sati or Shakti

Lord Shiva is the one God who had a regular family and in fact had to marry twice — since the first wife Sati or Shakti — committed suicide due to some peculiar circumstances.

The first time it was Sati — the daughter of Prajapati Daksh, a psychic son of Brahma and his wife Prusuti — who was the daughter of the first Manu, known as Syambhu Manu — or the one who created himself and was said to be Brahma himself, who split his body into two and the male part became Syambhu Manu and the female part Shatrupa. These two then populated the world on Brahma's command. Syambhu Manu and Shatrupa had three daughters and two sons — the youngest Rasuti was married to Daksh, as already mentioned. This couple had sixteen daughters, out of them thirteen were married to Dharm and one to Agni, one to Patris and the youngest Sati was married to Lord Mahadev. Daksh did not very much like the idea of marrying his daughter to one who had such gross looks and who roamed around cremation ground and kept the oddest company. Still Sati had her heart set on Mahadev and Brahma also encouraged 'Daksh' to do so, as Mahadev was one of the holy Trinity!

Sati and Mahadev lived happily in their abode at Mt. Kailash. Sati was not such a docile creature and had a mind of her own and often did not listen to her husband. She did what she herself wanted to, in spite of his telling her not to do so!

Once as they were riding around on 'Nandi' the bull to see if the world was functioning as ordained. They came across two handsome youths walking around in the forest, looking woebegone and extremely anxious. Seeing them Lord Shiva bowed his head and folded his hands in a *namaskar* saying. "It seems Vishnu has taken Ram avtar already." Sati asked him what he meant by that because if one of the youths according to him was Vishnu himself, why is he despondent? "Because Ram's wife Sita has been carried away by Ravan, the King of Lanka, and Ram is searching for her in desperation" said Shiva, "If that be so why Vishnu — who is Omniscient and knows the future, be so unhappy"? Mahadev just smiled — Sati was not satisfied and decided to test the youths. She changed herself into a look-a-like of Sita, and stood in the path of Ram and Laxman. Laxman was puzzled — but not Ram. He bowed and with folded hands asked Sati (in the garb of Sita): "Mother, why are you alone in this dense forest, and where is Shivji?" — thus proving to her that he was really Vishnu — Sati ran back to her husband who was just about to sit down for meditation. Still He asked her, "What is the result of your research?" He quickly told him an untruth and said that she had actually believed him and did not really test the youths! Mahadev knew the actual fact and told her so. He said, "Now that you had taken the garb of Sita who is Laxmi herself and is like a mother to me, I cannot accept you as my wife, therefore, your seat from now on is not on my left, but in front of me — as that is the place to a mother". Sati was aghast at this pronouncement, but could do nothing about it. She accepted her husband's decision, although she was heart broken. One day while sitting thus she saw a lot of *vimans* (aeroplanes) carrying devtas and rishis and their wives dressed very well and in great excitement flying past overhead. She looked up and asked Shivji as to where all those people were going. Shivji had also got up from his meditation because of the noise, and inquired from one of his doots (the server) as to the cause of such activity. The 'doot' informed him that Daksh has been given the title of 'Prajapati' (progenitor of the human race) and he is celebrating this honour by holding a great *yagya* known as 'Brishaspati Sava' at Kankhal near Haridwar. Sati was surprised that she and her husband had not been invited, but was very keen to go, as she felt that it was her father's house and she really didn't need an invitation! She said to Shivji, "Your father-in-law, my father has begun to perform a great yagna. We should also go there. We are his children. All the devtas and rishis are there with their wives. People are still going in that direction so it is evident that it is not yet over and I want to go there my Lord — I want to meet my mother and my sisters. I am very eager to go and see the yagya."

Mahadev told her that if it was any other person he would have gone but Daksh had purposely not invited them because at the yagna known as 'Brahma Satra' which was being performed by Marichi and other great sages sometime back Daksh who had already been chosen for the title of Prajapati by Brahma came in with great pride, shining like the Sun in all its glory. Everyone got up and He (Shiva) did not. This annoyed Daksh very much, as Daksh took it as an insult for not being honoured by his own son-in-law, quite forgetting that Shiva was one of the Holy Trinity. So full of ego he was that from that day he refused to honour Shiva.

Sati was still keen to go and so she went. On reaching there her father did not welcome her at the gate where he stood welcoming all others. Only her mother and sisters came forward to embrace her. The rest were frightened of Daksh and kept quiet. Sati also saw that no one asked her the reason for her husband's absence. There was no 'Havis' or portion for Shivji (the offerings that are first taken out in honour of each God).

The insult to her in not even recognising her as a daughter of the house was bearable, but the insult to her husband the 'Great God' was too much to her. She loved and honoured

Him far too much and her anger towards her father was also too much for her. Shiva had forsaken her as a wife and she felt quite unwanted, so she in her rage jumped into the sacrificial fire and burnt herself to death.

There was great chaos at the yagna as soon as Shivji heard of it. He was furious and brought forth a terrible being named 'Veerabhadra' and alongwith him and His own army of ghosts and spirits attacked the yagshala and played havoc with the assembly. He took the body of Sati on his shoulder and would not let it go. With flaming eyes he in his wrath nearly destroyed the world. All the devtas and the people cried out to Vishnu for help. Vishnu, realising the gravity of the situation, hurled his 'Sudharshan Chakra' and cut up Sati's body into twelve pieces; each piece fell down to the earth. Each place on which any part of the body fell became a holy 'shrine' and is known as a 'Shakti Peetha'. Once the body was removed from Shiva's shoulder, he calmed down at the instance of Brahma and Vishnu and returned to Mt. Kailash leaving the people of the earth to return back to their routine and did not bother about them for a lomg time. Thus ended Shiva's first marriage in disaster.

After the terrible uprooting of the great yagna and the indifference of Mahadev to the world it greatly upset the devtas. The gods went to Brahma to seek his advice. Brahma accompanied them and convinced Shiva that he being the 'Almighty' Himself, was nobleness and forgiveness personified. Any oblation offered to any God or devta was actually His. Shankar being 'Bholanath' (simple person) forgave everyone and shed his aloofness from the worlds which was suffering due to His neglecting it.

The yagna of Daksh — which could not be left half way — was completed with dignity and honour. Daksh lost his pride and had to wear a goat's head from then on. Vishnu came and told the assembly that He, Brahma and Shiv were actually one and no one should forget that and so peace returned to the three worlds.

Parvati or Uma

Parvati or Uma

When Sati threw herself in the fire she had asked the holy fire to make her Shivji's wife again in her next birth. Sati was then born as a daughter to the great King of the Himalayas King Himavant and his wife Maina. She was named Girja, Uma or Parvati meaning the daughter of the mountains.

Somehow, she was from childhood fascinated with Shiva and often went and placed flowers and incense at His shrine. Narad Muni knew the destiny of this little girl and would also often go and praise Mahadev to her. He told her parents on seeing her horoscope that she was a divine being and her husband would be immortal. They will be the most devoted couple in the whole universe. But to convince Shiva was a more difficult task as He had become absolutely unapproachable. So Indra was sent to the God of love Kamdev to do something about it. Kamdev took the spring season with him to the mountain home of Shiva and soon enough the spring turned the snowclad peaks into a beautiful garden with trees and shrubs full of flowers and fruits and nature became joyful and romantic. Shiva seeing this change opened his eyes and at that moment Kamdev shot an arrow of love at Shiva — but Shiva woke up and sent a lightning streak from his third eye towards Kamdev. Kamdev's body got immediately burnt, he remained alive in his spirit form. This was terrible for his wife Rati. She could do nothing about it, but made Shiva promise that Kamdev will regain his body

as Pradyuman, the son of Lord Krishna in 'Dwapar Yug'.
Shiva went back to his meditation.

Uma fell more and more in love with Shiva as she grew
up to be a beautiful young woman. On the advice of sage
Narad and others, she decided to do *tapasya* to obtain Him.
She started living a life of austerity and worship of Shiva to
convince Him of her love. Lord Shiva in the meantime had
been convinced by the sages and devtas that he must marry
as without a consort his shakti would vanish, and no one
was better suited than Uma, the daughter of Himavant —
so one day He came to test her and on seeing her
worshipping Him, he in the guise of a mendicant told her
horrible tales of Shiva and his way of life and his associates,
but Parvati was adamant. Lord Shiva came into his own form
then and offered to marry her and live with her forever.

Narad and other sages were sent to 'Himavant' who
called Parvati and asked her in front of all of them if she
agreed to marry Shiva. She looked down at the lotus in her
hand and started counting the petal in her shyness —
Himavant consented to the marriage. The *baraat* came in
the style of Shiva on the appointed day. Maina the mother
was taken aback when she saw the *baraat* but did the 'arta'
and accepted Shambhu (as Shiva was also called) alongwith
his snakes and frightful companions. Shiva and Paravati —
the eternal couple — then went to Kailash in happiness and
love.

Parvati soon became the symbol of worship of all
unmarried and married women of the world. She was a very
benevolent Goddess and was particular in bestowing boons
to unmarried girls as they prayed to her for husbands of their
choice or dreams, also to married women who prayed to her
to give long life to their husbands on whom depended
everything after their marriage. The women chose Parvati,
who was loved very very much by her husband and gave
her the name of 'Gauri' or Gaura, to whom they prayed to
on 'Karva-Chouth' with much devotion.

Parvati became the custodian of women and was equated to all the Goddesses that were to come later 'Shakti' was another name of the Goddess as she and Sati or Shakti are the same essentially — but Shakti is usually used as a name for Sati. Shakti is power — and the consorts of the Gods are their power. Therefore, without Shakti, all Gods are static.

Ambika or Durga is supposed to be born of the body of Parvati and thus Parvati became the essence of all forms of the mother Goddess like Ishani, Aparna, Gauri, Gaura, Durga, Tara, Kali, Vaishnav Devi, Ambika, Chaumandi, Annpurna, etc., etc. They were attributed with different temperaments and forms. The stories connected to their doings and to their appearance at different times depending on situations — are all absorbed very naturally, by the Hindus. She is the power of the Gods which can manifest itself in any form and at any time. This again is in the genius of the Hindu faith to manifest the unmanifest for the sake of getting it accepted by all and sundry in forms which they had somehow already accepted due to fright or love.

Parvati, therefore, is as complex as her spouse 'Lord Shiva'. She can be fearsome being as Kali or most benevolent as Durga or Gauri. The temples of Parvati alone are never there, she is always with Shivji, but in the form of Durga, Kali and others. She stands alone and is worshipped as such all over the country. More people seem to have faith in Her than in the male Gods.

Parvati also got mixed up with Yogmaya whom Krishna had given a 'Vardan' to be worshipped as Devi in all her manifestations during the end of Dwapar. They are essentially the Unmanifest power of the universe, so they are really one in their different manifestations and with Brahma, Vishnu and Mahesh who are the functioning deities, Devi became the 'power' that gives them the drive to do so, yet all is One.

Shiva and Parvati had no children as a couple, although Kartik and Ganesh are accepted as Shiva's and Parvati's sons. Their birth is attributed to strange circumstances, in which only one of them was involved. The details I shall put in the chapter concerning these two.

Kartikeya

Kartikeya

The elder son of Lord Shiva — Kartikeya — was not born of either Sati, His first wife, nor of Parvati, His second wife. His first wife Sati had killed herself by jumping into the fire of the *yagya* her father was performing in celebration for getting the title of 'Prajapati'. She could not bear the insult to her husband by her father, who even denied him the 'Havis' due to every God when a *havan* is performed — in fact, he had not even invited Shiva and Parvati for the great occasion.

Lord Shiva was extremely unhappy at the death of His beloved wife and created great havoc in the three worlds by dancing the 'tandav' to destroy everyone and everything in His anger. He returned to the mountains after Vishnu succeeded in calming Him down, but refused to marry again.

Sati had in the meantime taken birth as Parvati in the home of Himavant and Maina, the King of Himalayas. As a child even she became very devoted to Shivji — mainly on the coaxing of the Narad Muni, who knew that she was a 'Divine Being' and was to be the wife of Shiva. Naradji convinced her parents also by reading it in her horoscope and palm. Parvati decided to do *tapasya* to charm Lord Shiva, who was paying no attention to her or to anyone else for that matter.

The Gods and devtas were also in a hurry for them to marry, because they were being greatly harassed by a terrible demon named 'Tarak' — who had succeeded in pleasing Lord Brahma in granting him great powers, by his single-minded devotion to the easily pleased Lord of Creation. The powers that this demon mastered could not be overcome by anyone not even Brahma Himself. This Tarak started to disturb the rhythm of the seasons and scattered the offering meant for the demi Gods and devtas. This was very disturbing for the three worlds. The devtas went to Brahmaji who declared his inability to do anything to one to whom He himself has given unconquerable powers, but he declared that when Shiva and Parvati marry and have a son, he will destroy this demon. Hence the hurry to get Shiva out of His unhappy state and get Him married quickly.

They then took the help of Kamdev, the God of love, but the poor chap got burnt in the process by Shiva's third eye — therefore, although he lives because Rati — his wife — pleaded with Shiva so much, still he has lost his body for all times and is invisible.

Shivji in the meantime was being persuaded by Vishnu and Narad to get married for the good of the world and seeing the devotion of Parvati and after testing her love for Him, he eventually married her. They were very much in love. After even a thousand years of 'love play' as the scriptures call their honeymoon, they were unable to have a child. The devtas got very panicky, and asked Shiva for His seed, so that they could plant it in another womb. Agni agreed to take it and in the shape of a pigeon took it into herself, but due to its great power she could not retain it and threw it in the Ganges. It got dissolved into the water and entered the body of six women — the wives of six rishis — who were bathing in the Ganga. Their husbands turned them out on the charge of adultery and they had to go and live in the mountains, where in due course they gave birth each to a part of a baby. They didn't know what to do with the six parts and threw them back into the Ganga but the Ganga could not bear the load and went to Vishnu, who advised her to throw them on the reed grass on its bank. There the six parts came together on the 6th day of the 'Sukul Paksh' in the month of Masgshirsha (September–October) and Lord Shiva's son was born of six women — a very handsome child but he had six faces. A divine being named 'Karthika' took him under her wing and thus he became known as Kartikeya.

Uma one day asked Shiva as to what had happened to the seed which He had given to Agni? On realising that they had no information about it, they both got worried, as the seed of one of the Holy 'Trinity' cannot be wasted. They soon found out from the demi-Gods how the seed was instrumental in bringing forth a child, named Kartikeya and this child was being brought up by a divine woman.

Both Shiva and Parvati in great happiness went and fetched their son to Mt. Kailash. It is said that Parvati was really very unhappy about not being able to bear a child herself and was angry with the Gods for having implanted Shiva's seed into another woman's womb, so she cursed all the other two divine wives that they also will never be able to have children. That is why both Saraswati and Laxmi have no children of their very own. Kartikeya came to be known as Shadanand or Shadarupa (the six faced one). In the South of India he is called lovingly as Murugan or Subramanyan, the first meaning one who rides a peacock (which is his vahan) and the second because he had a very good and lovely fair complexion. He was a very good-looking child and grew up to be a very handsome young man. Because Agni had first tried to bear him, he is also known as Agnibhooshank. Skand is another popular name for him earned when he fought and defeated Inder — the chief of the devtas. He was also in the reeds on the banks of the Ganga. Therefore, some call him 'Saravanabhoo' or 'Sarojanman' synonymous with the name of the 'grass Saravana' — which grew on the banks of the sacred river.

The devtas came to Shiva and asked the Lord for the loan of his elder son to kill the demon Tarak. The demon was soon vanquished by Kartik and he was appointed the Commander-

in-Chief of the army of all the devtas for all times. His fame
spread far and wide and reached the king of Kronch (Heron),
who wanted him to kill 'Banasur', great destructive demon.
He killed 'Banasur', a demon who lived on 'Krauncha
Mountain'. He liked the place so much that he settled there
in the deep south and later made it his home after his tiff
with his parents.

He became so famous as a warlord that he was equated
to the planet Mars — the one that is the warlord amongst
planets.

Kartikeya and Ganesh lived very happily together with
their parents and were very fond of each other, but there
seems to have cropped up a problem, the result of which
some scriptures say was that Ganesh was married off earlier
while Kartikeya was away taking a round of the world along
with other Gods so as to be appointed the first amongst the
gods to be worshipped if he stood first. Ganesh in the
meantime won the race by taking a round of his parents who
were the world to him! And that annoyed Kartikeya so much
that he refused to stay with his parents any more, and left
for the south and made his home on the Kraunch mountain
beyond the river Narbada and there became a favourite
'God' of the South. In South he is referred to as the younger
son of Shiva and Parvati and is shown as married to a woman
known as Kumari or Devasena or Valli, but in the North he
is shown as never been married. Perhaps his anger with his
parents while he was in the North — left the North Indians
believing that he never did marry! — but he seems to have
thawed when in the South and got married. In the North it
is reputed that he does not like women and hence women
were not allowed in his temple. In any case, there are no
temples dedicated to him in the North of India. He never
came back to Kailash or Kashi, the abode of Lord Shiva and
Parvati but they still go to visit him — Parvati on the full moon
night of every month and Shiva on the new moon night.

As said before Kartik is one of the most popular Gods of the South. He is worshipped with much fervour on 'Skand Shasthi' in the Tamil month of Tulam (October–November). He is seen holding an arrow in one hand and a bow in the other. Here he is also known as Kumar — Mahasena — Senapati — Sidda — Sena, Siddha Swami — Yudha-dhara, Guhya (the mysterious one) Shakti-dara — Dwaadas Kakasha (twelve-eyed).

He has a lot of temples dedicated to him in the South of India. On 'Skand Shasthi' the devotees rush from one temple to another in their effort to reach as many as possible and please the Lord. This day is observed as the day he killed the demon 'Tarak' for whose destruction he was born and became also known as Tarakjit. Even in the South his image is always shown along with other Gods although he occupies the middle spot.

In Bengal also Kartik is worshipped and recognised as the handsomest of the demi Gods. On Durga Puja — he has to be worshipped along with Ganesh and Durga Ma.

Kartik can be shown holding a bow, an arrow — a conch — a rose and even a sword in one hand, the other hand is always shown as of giving a blessing and is held with the palm up in a gesture of giving a boon. His vehicle is a peacock.

Lord Ganesh

Lord Ganesh

L ord Ganesh — the second son of Shiva and Parvati — is the one with the elephant head and a round bulging stomach. He is the God who is to be worshipped before any other deity, even before the worship of Shiva, Brahma and Vishnu. He is the God of progress and enlightenment. He removes all obstacles and, therefore, any and all auspicious occasions like a marriage, childbirth, buying a house or building or even starting on a journey, the name of Ganesh is invoked first, only then the other rituals or work are started. He is a very benevolent God, but if not respected can put a lot of obstacles in the way. He is very wise and the love of people has given him many different names. He is called as:

Varasiddhi Vinayak — This aspect is worshipped on Ganesh Chaturthi.

Ganesh or Ganaadhipati or Ganpati — This means the leader of a group and since he is worshipped before any other deity — he is automatically the leader (Ganna means a group of people and pati means the leader).

Vighnashar — Standing on a demon named Vighnasura whom he had killed.

Uma Putar — The son of Uma.

Vinayak — A great leader and hence he has four hands in which he holds the symbol.

Ekadanta — The one with one tooth.

Lambodar — With a bulging stomach.
Vighneshwar — One who controls all obstacles.
Musikvaachan — He who rides on a mouse.
Sarva-Siddhamta — Who provides all kinds of Siddhi's.
Gajaanana — Elephant head.
Heramba — Favourite of the mother.

He is also sometimes attributed with being a master of dance because he is supposed to have danced once when he saw Lord Vishnu who bowed to him and which pleased him greatly and thus he is depicted as Natta Ganapati. There are many other names like Vikat Shakti Ganapati — shown with Riddhi and Siddi, his wives, as his powers with him or even Buddhi (knowledge) or Laxmi sitting on his thigh. Worship of these aspects grants your wishes very quickly.
Bara Ganapati and Taruna Ganapati — depicts him as child and a young man.
Gajamukh — elephant face.
Herambeganapathe — He has five heads and ten arms, three eyes in each face and rides a lion.
Vinan Vignesh — Depicts his martial spirit and carries a lot of weapons in his ten hands.

The birth of Lord Ganesh has many legends connected to it, different purans carry different tales of his birth, as different rishis wrote them and perhaps at different places and different times not really knowing where Ganesh came from, but his birth is celebrated on Ganesh Chaturthi on the 4th day of the moonlit night in the month of Bhado (September). Shiva and Parvati really could not conceive although they had tried to do so for a thousand years — hence both Kartik — the elder son is attributed to Shiva alone, and Ganesh to Parvati only. The Hindu accepts the imagination with the actual with equal ease since it does not interfere with the true essence of the Hindu philosophy, —

they do not argue about the frills that the ancient thought necessary for protection and interest of the masses. They good-humouredly accept all versions.

The most accepted theory of Ganeshji's birth is that once Shivji went off to the mountains for samadhi (meditation) leaving Parvati at Kailash (or some say at her mother's house at Kashi). Parvati used to have her bath in a place where there was no door, so she decided to make a child from the scruff of her body and stationed him at the entrance to stop anyone from entering, while she was bathing. The beautiful child she made stood obediently at the door. He was about 10 or 12 years of age.

One day when Shivji returned from Kailash He went looking for his wife and on being told that she was having a bath, made straight for her chamber. He found a young boy guarding the entrance and not knowing him at all, Shiva brushed him aside and tried to enter. The boy stood firm in his way. He also held a staff in his hand and with its help stopped Shivji from going in. This greatly annoyed Shiva and in anger told the boy to step aside. The boy said, "No one can enter while my mother bathes". Shivji angrily told him something like this, "Do you know who I am? I am Shankar, the owner of this house and in fact the whole world and you dare to stop me — the husband of Parvati!!" The boy replied: "I've never seen you before and I don't recognise you, I have been instructed by my mother — Parvati — to stop anyone from entering her chamber, I am her son Ganesh". Shivji looked shocked and told him that he had no son by the name of Ganesh and tried to push him aside several times, but the child was very strong and would not budge. This enraged Shivji all the more and he with his trident cut off the boy's head.

In some purans it is also said that Shivji called all his 'ganas', his servants, and fought a battle with Ganesh but they along with Shiva were injured badly. Narad who roams around freely in the three worlds saw this great struggle and rushed to Brahma, who came to the venue. After announcing as to who he was he told the boy that Shiva was really his father and the husband of Parvati but Ganesh pulled Brahma's beard and even injured him. Brahma had to leave in great bewilderment at the strength of this boy. In a way Brahma was Ganesh's grandfather, as Sati, the first wife of Shiva, was Daksh's daughter and Daksh was Brahma's son and Parvati was the incarnation of Sati. Vishnu then came and tried to placate the boy, but got hurt in the bargain. At last Shiva's trident did the trick, although his famous bow was broken (known as Pinaate) in the melee.

All this while, Parvati was still having her bath. She heard the noise as she came into her chamber to dress and on seeing Ganesh's head severed from his body and that too by Shiva's trident, she got mighty angry with her husband and told him in no uncertain terms that first having left her alone, and made her suffer His absence and then to return without notice and kills His own son was unforgiveable. She started such a lament, that her husband could not hear her anger and sorrow. In the meantime, one of the 'Ganas' had run off with Ganesh's head and it could not be found, but Parvati would not rest in peace. So Shivji declared that the first living thing that came that way will give his head to Ganesh body and He Himself will do the needful. The first living thing that came that way was an elephant; so it was that Ganesh got the head of an elephant. Seeing her son looking like an elephant made Parvati all the more upset. She started to wail all the more and told Shiva: "No one will worship my son as a God, you have made him look like an elephant". Shivji, being God almighty, declared there and then that from that day onwards no one can worship any other God before Ganesh was worshipped first. That decree holds for all times and for all shades of Hindus. Lord Shiva is also the protector of the animals which is amply testified as one finds that 'Shiva' is worshipped in animal form of Pashupati (the leader of animals). Therefore, a son of his with an animal face is quite in keeping with the Hindu philosophy that all are part of the same Supreme Spirit.

There is another story which says that once all the Gods had an argument as to who amongst them (the demi-Gods) was to be the first 'demi-God'? It was decided to have a race to solve this problem and whoever went round the world first should be declared as the first God to be worshipped. So it was that everyone got their vehicles and Ganesh's elder brother Kartik also took off on his peacock. Ganesh was on his mouse, a very slow vehicle indeed. So what Ganesh did was to make his parents sit down together and after doing *namaskar* to them, went round them on his mouse, and finished before any of the others had returned. He then declared that as it is so written in the shastras that 'parents' are to be considered the whole world to a person, he had circled them and, therefore, he had won the race. This impressed everyone and Ganesh became the first God of the Hindu pantheon.

Since Ganesh was not beautiful he had difficulty in getting married, while all the other gods were being sought after. He got very angry and told the rats to dig up holes on any path that the *baraat* of any God would go to the bride's house thus creating a lot of potholes and obstacles in their way. The poor Gods as grooms got very rattled and could not go elegantly for their marriage. They all went to Brahma and complained bitterly about Ganesh and his tricks. Brahma accosted Ganesh and asked him as to why he was creating obstacles in the marriage of the demi Gods? Ganesh told Brahma his own problem as he also wanted a wife. Brahma then created two beautiful girls — one Riddi (Prosperity) and the other Siddi (Success) — and told Ganesh he can have two wives instead of one and Brahma along with Saraswati gave away these girls in marriage to Ganesh, thus also becoming his father-in-law in the process. Ganesh then told the rats to stop their digging and became known as the vanquisher of all obstacles and made the rat his *vahan* in appreciation.

Ganesh is very fond of eating *ladoos* and other sweetmeats and can never resist them. Once at night he found a lot of them and just could not stop eating, sure enough his stomach burst and the ladoos came out. The moon which used to be then always full and beautiful could not help laughing. This annoyed Ganesh very much and he in his temper cursed the moon that he will from then on never be able to hold his beautiful face since he was so proud of it!! and ever since then the moon is waxing and wanning all the time.

One finds Ganesh very much loved, and in different regions he is worshipped in his different stages. In the North it is mainly as a child but in Maharashtra where He is the principal "God" he is worshipped as a mature and very wise person. 'Ganesh Chaturthi' is the biggest festival of that region. It is celebrated at home as well as publicly.

Ganesh was appointed by Narad as the scribe to Ved Vyas to pen down the 'Mahabharat' and the 'Bhagwat' because of His deep understanding of the meaning of the slokas. Ved Vyas could dictate without pausing or correcting him. Ganesh wrote these both with his broken tooth.

Now to tell you how Ganesh lost his one tooth. He now always carries it in one hand. Once Ganesh approached Brahma, Vishnu and Mahesh to make him immortal, but Parashuram who was himself immortal, took exception to this and wanted to test him as he thought Ganesh did not fulfil the conditions necessary for immortality. Both get very angry with each other and this caused a big battle which Ganesh lost as Parashuram was very strong. Parashuram also broke one of Ganesh's two teeth with his axe, so now Ganesh carries it around in his hand.

He, of course, gave up the idea of becoming immortal. Still all Hindus love Him and without fail worship him first and always have an image or picture of him in the house.

Even at the entrance one finds the image of Ganesh welcoming one to the house where He resides in love and glory to bring prosperity and success.

Ganesh is usually shown with four hands, each having a different symbolic object in it. In one hand he has an Ambush (a goad), the second has a trishul (a three-pronged weapon) or an axe made from his broken tooth, the third has a lotus and the fourth has a rosary. He always has a tiara or a crown on his head and a belt round his stomach to keep the garments from slipping off his bulging stomach. The belt is in the form of a snake which He inherits from his father Lord Shiva.

Any image with the trunk of Ganesh pointing to the right is always for worship and the one pointing to the left can be decorated in the house. The practice is to do *namaskar* everyday to any image which has been put as a decoration piece but has its trunk pointing to the right. One should burn an *agarbati* or any incense near it now and then.

The sign of the swastika is an age-old sign of the Aryan race. In India it is now symbolised with Ganesh. All auspicious drawings for puja or any other auspicious occasions have the swastika or a small image of Ganesh on top of the page.

Lord Hanuman

Lord Hanuman

The most worshipped and remembered demi God —
especially in time of trouble or danger — is Lord
Hanuman. It is quite normal for a Hindu, howsoever
educated he or she may be — to invoke the name of
Hanuman whenever in distress, and offer *prasad* to the deity
as soon as the danger or fear has passed.

Hanumanji has never claimed to be a God, but calls
himself the most faithful and devoted servant of Ram, an
avtar of Vishnu in the 'Treta Yug'. Hanumanji, as He is
lovingly called by all Hindus, is not even supposed to be a
human being, but a monkey who met Ram and Laxman
while they were searching for Sita — the wife of Ram who
had been kidnapped by Ravan, the King of Sri Lanka. He
most probably belonged to a tribe who looked like monkeys.
After that he became the greatest *Bhakt* of Ram and Sita.
He is always there with one who praises Ram and Sita. They
say that a seat must always be prepared for him and kept
empty in any place where 'Ram Charitra Manas' is being
read or a gathering of 'Ram Bhakts' gather to sing His praise.
He will rush to help anyone who prays to him sooner than
any other God, and is easily pleased or annoyed. One has
to be careful and offer *prasad* in his temple as soon as the
desire of the person is fulfilled or he might get angry and
send a monkey to remind one of the promise made to him.
The monkey may just jump on a tree or sit on a roof without
harming anyone, but it is true that if a monkey is paying

special attention to you, it means you have forgotten to offer *prasad* in a Hanuman temple as promised earlier.

Hanumanji was the chief lieutenant of Sugreev, a prince who had been ousted by his elder brother Bali from Kishkunda (Bastar in Madhya Pradesh) from their kingdom, in the mistaken belief that Sugreev had usurped the throne while Bali was fighting with a demon and consequently was absent from the kingdom for quite a while. According to an agreement between the two brothers, Sugreev would ascend the throne if Bali did not return after a stipulated period. Bali got late in coming and found his brother on the throne. This angered him so much that instead of understanding that it was his own fault, he threw Sugreev out of the kingdom with some of the latter's faithful followers. Bali also took Sugreev's wife as one of his own.

So Sugreev lived in constant fear of his brother and hid himself in the jungles of Kishkunda. He was afraid of any one who ventured near his hide out. On seeing the two youths coming that side, he sent Hanuman to find out if they were spies of Bali! On learning that they were the sons of Raja Dasrath, he welcomed them with great honour. Ram was naturally very sympathetic with Sugreev on hearing of Bali having taken Sugreev's wife as his own Sita had been taken by Ravan. They decided to wage a war with Bali, in which Ram killed Bali surreptitiously by hiding behind a tree and shooting an arrow when Bali's back was turned towards him. Although Bali went to heaven straight because he had been killed by Vishnu Himself, still he asked Ram before he died as to the unethical method that was employed in killing him. The reply was that taking a woman against her wishes was the greatest of crimes in the scriptures and all methods were justified in bringing the culprit to a just end. Well, this incident is even today a very controversial subject and in the eyes of many has lowered the prestige of Ram, and is being still argued by great philosophers, some in defence of the act and some against it. We will leave it for them to argue till times end as to the right and wrong of it!!

Hanuman took to Ram with such devotion that even when Sugreev was crowned king, he forsaked his allegiance to him and could think of nothing else except to serve Ram and Sita in every way possible and always remained with Ram.

Hanuman's birth is a mystery and no one exactly knows who his father was. Of course, Anjani is his mother and she was the wife of Kesari and both were faithful to Sugreev and lived in the jungles during Sugreev's banishment, but Hanumanji is described as Shankar Suvan (son of Shankar) or *Vayu putra* (son of Vayu) or Shivji Himself in the garb of Hanuman. He is even portrayed as Ram's brother.

In the Shiv Puran and some other scriptures, it is mentioned that during the churning of the ocean, Lord Vishnu had to take the form of a beautiful woman named 'Mohini' to enchant the 'asurs' and lure them away while the devtas took the 'amrit' to make them immortal. Lord Shiv was very susceptible to the charms of beautiful women. During this incident He also ran after Mohini in his sexual lust, but prematurely ejaculated. The seed of Shiva was too precious to be wasted, so the sages collected it in some leaves and later implanted it into Anjani's womb. Hanuman was thus born and is Shankar's son.

Another legend relates that Shiva was very keen to witness the *leelas* of Lord Vishnu as Ram on the earth. Ravan, as a great *bhakt* of Lord Shiva, had got boons from Him whereby he could not be killed by anyone of the gods or devtas. He wasn't concerned about the danger from the human race and the animals, as he could easily ·conquer them. Therefore, Ram came as a human being and Shiva decided to be a monkey and help Ram to kill Ravan who had become a demon. Shivji realised his mistake in granting him the boon. Shiva is also the God of all animals; therefore, it did not bother him to take the form of a monkey. He stayed

very close to Ram, after he became acquainted with him in
the guise of Hanuman.

One more legend in the Anand Ramayan tells the story
of an apsara named Suvarchala, who tried to entice the
creator Himself. Brahma cursed her to become a vulture and
on her pleading relented and told her that in Treta Yug, she
could steal some *kheer* from the portion of Keikeys' and then
would become the beautiful 'apsara' again. That *kheer*
contained the seed that had the *ansha* of the Almighty. It
happened as predicted but this apsara in the form of the
vulture could not carry this *kheer* in her beak as it proved
too hot. She dropped it in the forest of Kishkunda where
Anjani got hold of it and ate it up. Hanuman was born to
her because of the *kheer*. Thus he became a brother of Ram,
Laxman, Bharat and Shatrughan.

The fourth legend describes 'Vayu' as having embraced
Anjani and getting her pregnant, since Anjani and Kesari
could not conceive as a couple. Anjani was reincarnation
of a sage's wife who had unwittingly got cursed by her
husband to become a monkey in Treta Yug and would be
only redeemed by having 'Hanuman' as her son. 'Vayu Dev'
gave her a boon that he will father a son for her as Kesari
was not able to. Thus Anjani agreed on the advice of a sage
named Matange. This is a story featured in the Vaishnava
section of the 'Skand Puran' and also in the 'Valmiki
Ramayan' and is the most accepted version of today.

Kesari of course accepted Hanuman as his son without
fuss as was the custom of those times.

The birthday of Hanumanji is celebrated on the full moon
night of Chait somewhere between 15th of March and 15th
April. When the child was born Anjani named him Sunder
as he had the most beautiful physique. He was a very strong
child in any case.

Once as a baby, Sunder was left alone sleeping in a
cave. He woke up and found no one there. He was feeling
very hungry and could find nothing in the cave to eat. He

looked out and saw the Sun just coming out, looking like a red fruit. Since Vayu was his father and he could fly easily he flew right up to the Sun and gobbled it up and there was complete darkness in the three worlds. The Gods got very disturbed and tried to get the Sun out of Sunder's mouth but the boy charged at them — even with his mouth full. Indra threw his thunderbolt on him which hit him on his chin and made him dislodge the Sun. Although the chin later healed yet it has still got a bit out of shape. Of course, the wind God was very angry and stopped blowing his breeze which made the Gods very uncomfortable and the inhabitants of the world could hardly breathe. The gods then assured Vayu that his son Hanuman would be the strongest being in the three worlds and shall be immortal as the other sages and they — the gods — would never try to get the better of him, if Vayu gave them their breath back and again cooled the three worlds with its breeze. Brahma was also there and He named him Hanuman; He told the devtas that this child would play wonders on this earth to the amazement of even the gods. The child was given all the knowledges by the Sun God and the God Varun made him immune to water. Hanuman became extremely strong and was known as 'Bajrang Bali' (taken from Vajrang — the thunderbolt) while being taught by the Sun, he got so exposed to it that his skin got very tanned and his whole body became red in the process.

As a child Hanuman was very naughty although so very strong that he created problems for the 'rishis'. One of them cursed him by saying that He would become unconscious of his own strength from then on and until someone reminded him of it, he would feel like any other person in strength. He could also expand his body and become very tall and large, or diminish himself and became very tiny — at his will.

While staying with Sugreev after he became king of Kishkunda, Ram entrusted Hanuman with his own ring and sent him to Sri Lanka to inform Sita that he was closeby and that he would come soon to her rescue. Jamvant the bear reminded Hanuman of his strength and that he could fly as he was in a quandary as to how to cross the ocean. Soon Hanuman arrived at the abode of Sita, who was living in a small garden outside the capital of Sri Lanka. Ravan used to come everyday and trouble her, demanding her consent to marry him, which she has vehemently been refusing. Ravan had been cursed that if he took any woman by force, he would die. Therefore, he could not force her. Anyway, Hunuman dropped the ring into Sita's lap from a tree and introduced himself when she looked up. Soon with her permission he created havoc in the garden by eating up all the fruits and uprooting all the trees, etc. and creating chaos.

When caught by the men of Lanka and produced before Ravan it was decided to set fire to his tail, as a monkey loves his tail. Everyone was shocked to see Hanuman elongating his tail to such an extent that the fire never reached his body. Hanumanji then jumped on a tree and from there ran amuck all over Sri Lanka and burnt down the city which was reputed to be made of gold, so rich the Kingdom of Ravan was supposed to be.

Then he led Ram towards where his wife was imprisoned. Ram made war on Ravan, and during the war Laxman got hit by an arrow which killed him, and Hanuman was sent to Sri Lanka to bring the personal physician of Ravan 'Sushav'. The Vaidji prescribed the 'Sanjeevni booti' to resurrect Laxman. This 'booti' grew only on the 'Himalayas'. Hanuman was entrusted the task of bringing the booti (herb) from there. On reaching the Himalayas he could not distinguish the plant from the other herbs, so he brought the whole mountain to Lanka thus saving Laxman's life and earned the gratitude of Ram for all times. Ram declared that He himself could never never repay Hanuman for what he had done for him and from then on anyone who pleased 'Hanuman' would please him and reach Him at the end of life, all his or her sins would be forgiven.

'Hanumanji' was then sent to Ayudhya to inform the family and the people of Ayudhya that Ram had won the war against Ravan and would return with Sita and Laxman alongwith the whole tribe that had helped him and reach in twenty days' time after fourteen years of exile. Thus Dessara is the day of 'victory' for Ram at Sri Lanka and a day earlier to the 20th day, after Dessara. Hanumanji reached Ayudhya and gave the good news. The mothers of Ram and the brothers were overjoyed. They lighted lamps in and around their houses and paths. The next day was the day of revelry and joy and the whole of Ayudhya became a fairyland with every home lighted with earthen *diyas* and decorated and painted anew. There was much dancing and joy as Ram, Laxman and Sita arrived by the *Uran katolah* (airplane) which they took from Ravan's kingdom. It is said that Ravan had taken it by force from his half brother 'Kuber', the custodian of all the wealth of 'Aryavarta'. The day Ram, Sita and Laxman arrived at Ayudhya is celebrated as Diwali and comes after twenty days after Dessara.

Once when Hanuman saw Sita putting *sindhoor* on the parting on her hair, he asked her why she did so. She told him it was a token to show how much she loved Ram. Hanumanji could not wait for another moment and smeared *sindhoor* all over his body, face and arms. Ever since then his image is always covered with *sindhoor*, in every temple in the country.

When he was once asked where Ram and Sita resided, he tore open his chest and showed Ram and Sita sitting in his heart.

He is easily pleased and can do wonders and that too he does quickly. Therefore, the Hanuman Chalissa is a favourite with all Hindus and they chant it in time of danger or in prayer to Hanumanji from where they can get to Ram and Sita easier. He has become a very powerful God for all shades of Hindu and even people of other religions are seen asking Him for boons when in difficulty — Tuesday is his day. Even Sanni is soft towards him and accepts the prayer to Hanuman on this day with great devotion.

Hanuman is not married. He is shown with a gadda in one hand and the mountain in the other. His *Vahan* (vehicle) is the wind.

This aspect meant for the human being to realise that the animal world is as close to the heart of the Almighty as they are. There is always an underlying truth in all the stories concerning the Gods and demi-Gods and the Avtars and that is why they have withstood the test of time and are as alive as they were when conquered up.

The Matsaya Avtar
(Vishnu in the Form of Fish)

The Matsaya Avtar
(Vishnu in the Form of Fish)

A ll shades of Hindus believe that the Preserver Vishnu comes to earth in different forms — suitable to the time that the world needs at that period. The first four manifest forms — the unmanifest takes, are known as 'Bhogi'; they proceed slowly from the lowest animal form to the higher animal forms, in the soul's advancement for the fulfilment of its destiny. These four versions of life go more by instinct than brain power and slowly advance towards the human form developing the brain and later a 'conscience' to perfect itself for its ultimate aim of merging with the 'Eternal Spirit'.

After pralay when creation starts again, the first form that Vishnu takes is the form of a fish — known as the 'Matsaya avtar'.

One must know that the Hindu very easily mixes up the Gods and devtas and even human beings of the previous kalp or Manvantra in the building process of a new Creation. The legend is that in the previous 'Manvantra', just before the great deluge — a very noble and kind king named Satyavrata ruled the earth. Once when he was taking a bath on the banks of a river known as 'Kritamala', he took some water into his cupped hands to offer to the Sun God. He found a small fish in his hands, alongwith the water knowing that a fish is happiest in the water; he threw it back into the river. The fish spoke to him in a human voice and told him that it would rather stay with him because it was afraid that the big fish would eat it up in the river. It would like the king to take it with him. So the king put it in his kamandal and took it home. The king put her in a bowl of water but the next day he saw that the fish had grown bigger. On seeing Satyavrata it asked for more space. Satyavrata took it to a nearby pond and deposited it there. Next day the fish had grown even bigger than before and could not swim in the pond freely. The king found a larger pond for it but the same thing again happened: it grew bigger until the king decided to throw it back in the sea. The fish tried to argue with him, but Satyavrata told it that he was quite sure that it was no ordinary fish, and that it had some purpose behind all this 'leela'.

The fish having tested the king was now convinced that Satyavrata was a noble and kind man and the right one for it to disclose its true identity, and the purpose for its birth. The fish told Satyavrata that it was really the incarnation of Vishnu and had to take this form of life because *pralay* was about to deluge the world, and water would engulf everything. But the eternal rishis, herbs and seeds had to be saved for the next Manvantra. It warned Satyavrata that only seven days were left, and he will see great clouds in the horizon and the rains will fall in torrents and water will be everywhere. Narayan had chosen Satyavrata for the purpose of transferring the very essential items for the next "Creation". It also told Satyavrata that a boat will automatically come to him before everything is completely submerged, and he should by then have collected all the immortal rishis, plants and seeds, etc. and get into the boat alongwith these men and things. The fish which was Narayan himself will come to save them. The fish will have two horns, and Satyavrata with the consent of 'Vasuki' the serpent should use him as a rope and tie the boat to the horns of the huge fish. The boat will be tossed hither and thither, but he should not be afraid as the fish will guide him across to the next 'Manvantra'. Thus the first avtar of Narayan came in the form of a fish. It is in tune with the Darwin theory of evolution although woven around a story to keep everyone interested in listening to it.

This story is very akin to the story of the "Noahs' Arc" and seems to have its origin with the Aryans before they spread out from the Central Asia into the rest of the world.

Kurmi Avtar
(The Tortoise Avtar)

Kurmi Avtar
(The Tortoise Avtar)

T he second form of life that took its journey towards evolution was its efforts to come out of the waters and be able to exist on land. In this process came the 'Kurmi' avtar. The story connected with this *avtar* is as follows:

The devtas and asurs are not actually human beings, they are 'beings' that exist in other worlds, but are very much connected to the beings of this earth and very much interested in being the major influence on its inhabitants. They take part in all the issues connected with us, therefore, they are present at all the actions pertaining to us and are quite mixed up with all the *'avtars'* that chose to appear in our midst.

Therefore, at the time the world took shape they along with Brahma, Vishnu and Mahesh were all around and very active in the affairs of this new world, which was at that time — just water, water, everywhere and the fish appeared as the only living being.

The Gods and demi Gods and the devtas, who were all quite taken up with the building of this new habitat, decided to churn the ocean to get out all that lay underneath its hidden depths for the use of the species which were destined to inhabit this planet.

To churn the ocean they needed a big staff and a strong and long rope. Vishnu suggested that the great mountain

'Mandara' should be the churning staff and 'Vasuki' the serpent should be prevailed upon to become the rope. The mountain was very heavy and only Vishnu was able to lift it and set it on the ocean bed, because of its weight the mountain started to sink into the ocean floor. Narayan then took the form of a huge tortoise and took the weight of the mountain on his back which was a strong shield making it possible for the ocean to be churned.

Now the real interest of both the devtas and asurs was to get the *amrit* from the ocean and drink it. This nectar would make them immortal. That is why they whole-heartedly collaborated with each other. It is said that the asurs are always stronger than the devtas, and the Gods were not at all interested in letting the asurs become immortal! But their strength was needed to churn the mighty ocean, Vishnu told the devtas that he would see that the nectar only went to the devtas. Of course, it was only a part of the 'Preserver' that had taken the form of the tortoise. Vishnu in all His glory came on the side of the devtas. He soon succeeded in his getting the amrit to the devtas, by luring the asurs by transforming Himself into a beautiful woman named Mohini and except for one asur, Rahu, who had seen through the game succeeded in getting a few drops of it and became immortal. He was pointed out by the Sun God and the Moon God and quickly Vishnu cut him in two to try to destroy him, but Rahu had become immortal and could not be destroyed.

Both the parts became different identities and both became immortal and are now known as Rahu and Ketu. Now they trouble the Sun and the Moon by eclipsing them at intervals and the Sun and Moon suffer the humiliation for sometime every year.

The people of our world used to take out guns and fire blank shots at them or shout 'Rahu Ketu ke hattyare. Chandiama or Suraj devta ko chor.' (Rahu and Ketu you scoundreds leave the Moon or Sun God alone.)

Varaha Avtar

Varaha Avtar

After the evolument of an animal who could remain both in water and land, the process had to bring a form of life much more suitable to land, so came a life form which the Hindu believe to be the *avtar* of Vishnu in the form of a 'boar' or 'Varaha' which could swim but had four very mobile legs that helped it to walk and run on land with much ease and comfort. The Varaha preferred land to water and the stage of land specie came of age. Now the story:

At the time of creation when Manu approached his father Brahma, the Creator as to where he was supposed to make his progenies live, since after the *pralay* the earth had got submerged in the waters and there was no arrangement for the sustenance and homes for those that he had been commanded to create. Brahma was in a quandary. He thought of Narayan who had commanded him to populate the world again. Brahma asked him how the earth was to be brought out of the nether lands. As he was meditating on Lord Narayan, out of one of his nostrils came out a very tiny boar the size of a finger nail. It started to grow and grow and became a huge one. This was Vishnu Himself who came to help in establishing the world. He checked the water and then jumped into it — down to the very depth — where the earth was submerged. The Varah lifted it on to his two tusks and rose to bring it to the surface.

On the way he met the great 'asur' Hiranayksha — who had been one of the two gatekeepers of 'Vaikunt Lok', the residence of Lord Vishnu, their names had been Jaya and Vijaya. Once some rishis decided to meet the Lord and went to his abode — where they were not allowed to enter by Jaya and Vijaya blocking their way in their arrogance of being gatekeepers to the Lord Himself. This annoyed the rishis very much and they cursed the two to be born as asurs in 'Mrityu Lok'. Lord Vishnu came out to see what the commotion was about and seeing the 'rishis' He welcomed them with due humility — due to the learned — and on being told about the conduct of Jaya and Vijaya, He profusely apologised for their conduct and asked the 'rishis' to forgive them. Since no curse can be lifted completely, they modified it to the two being Asurs only for three *janams* and would only be killed by Vishnu, so that they returned to heaven but they were to hate the Lord in all their three *janams*, so much so that they would only think of Him all the time in their great hatred. They, however, would be redeemed before the end of Dwapar. Hiranyakashipu was one of them and was killed by the Lord in form of a boar — in his first *janam*. (The Lord took the form of Narasingha to kill Hiranyakashipu the other gate keeper).

The earth that came out of the nether world was beautiful and lovely and all the *devtas* sang the praise of the 'Almighty' and Manu and Shatroopa were pleased to populate it. The Adi Varah then vanished from the sight.

Narsimha or Narsingh Avtar

Narsimha or Narsingh Avtar

When Hiranyaksha was killed by Vishnu in his avtar as the Vara, his brother Hiranyakashipu was absolutely livid with rage and the thought that the one whom both the brothers had vowed to kill had in fact succeeded in killing one of them made him conscious of nothing else but how to finish off Narayan. In fact he dreamt of killing all the devtas and establishing asurs' raj in the land. All laws would be changed and life would be according to the 'asur' way. What was considered evil would be good, and good will become evil. He himself thought of taking the place of Brahma, but before that could happen he had to become all powerful.

His one great misfortune was his son Prahlad who instead of hating Narayan had become his ardent 'bakt'. So devoted was he to the Lord that even today no one can match him, though he was born an 'asur'. This was an intolerable situation for Hiranyakashipu. He tried his best to get his son killed by any means. He tried to throw him from a mountain — he tried to burn him — he dug a pit and buried him alive but to no avail and then he got him trampled by elephants, but the child seemed invincible and sang the praise of Narayan without fear.

Hiranyakashipu troubled the devtas so much that they had to run away from their abode. They disguised themselves as just anybody and moved from place to place without rest. The devtas then went to Brahma and warned him against being soft to the tyrant who had decided to please Brahma and was doing great *tapas* in honour of Brahma. Brahma went to the cave where the 'asur' was absorbed in meditation. He could not see Hiranya as he was covered with weeds and anthills. On seeing Brahma, Hiranyakashipu fell at his feet. Brahma was so overcome by the devotion and concentration of the asur that he was ready to give the 'asur' any boon he wanted, quite forgetting the warning of the devtas! Brahma soon sprinkled water on Hiranyakashipu from his *kamandal* and asked him as to what he wanted. The father of Prahlad asked Brahma to make him 'immortal'. Brahma told him that it was not in anybody's power to grant such a boon. Thereupon Hiranyakashipu asked him to grant that none of the power created by Him should be able to kill him nor should he die inside a house or outside one. Nor in the day or night should anyone be able to kill him. No man or animal should be the cause of his death, no living or non-living things should be able to kill him. No replite, devtas or asurs should be able to cause his demise. He also asked to be the wealthiest man on earth. Brahma granted him these wishes and vanished.

With all the boons granted Hiranyakashipu was able to conquer all the three worlds. The chief of the devtas Indra was made to wait on him. Even the earth and sea had to open their treasures to him and he became the most powerful being in the universe. Still he was not happy. He hated Narayan and could not rest in peace until he had killed Him.

Men and devtas prayed to the Lord in secret and when it became unbearable the devtas took courage and went to 'Vaikunt Lok' and entreated Vishnu to do something about it and that too as soon as possible. Realising the gravity of the situation Vishnu promised all that he would help them get rid of Hiran soon. Years were passing and inhabitants of the three worlds were terror struck to such an extent that they thought it would be better if *pralay* came.

In the meantime Hiranyakashipu tried his best to get his son to hate Narayan. He got two gurus to teach him the goodness of the 'asurs' and to make his son think that his father was the greatest person in the three worlds. The gurus tried three times to brainwash the child and each time failed. This angered the father so much that he himself tried to drive the 'Almighty' out of his son's brain. The son insisted that Narayan was everywhere. This made Hiranyakashipu all the more angry and he said: "If He is everywhere then produce him from this pillar of this room". So Prahlad prostrated himself before the pillar and declared that he saw the Lord inside there. The father in extreme anger told his son: "I am now going to kill you, let your Narayan save you this time" and he took out his sword and rushed towards Prahlad.

With a terrible noise the pillar split into two and out came a huge form glowing like gold with a face like a lion and the body of a very strong man. The awesome beast cannot be described, Hiranya was at first not afraid, but suddenly it dawned on him that the apparition was neither a man nor an animal and remembered that the boon given by Brahma, did not include such a thing! Still he rushed towards this half lion and half man. It was the Lord himself come to save Prahlad and the three worlds, and in spite of the asur trying to kill him with his mace the Lord caught him in his two mighty arms and carried him to the threshold of the hall, then placing the asur on his lap he tore his entails out with his nails and teeth killing him instantaneously. The time was twilight neither day nor night.

Hiranyakashipu was killed neither by a man nor an animal — not in the sky nor on earth (he was on the lap of the great beast that Narayan had chosen to become). Soon the Lord sat on the throne of Hiranya and looked so ferocious that all those present were frightened to see Vishnu in this form. The anger of the Lord could not be abated as this Hiranyakashipu had troubled his devotee — a little child — so very much. He could not be pacified by even Brahma or the devtas. Even Laxmi got frightened and could not do anything.

The whole assembly asked Prahlad to help and bring Narayan back to his usual calm self. Prahlad with tears flowing from his eyes pleaded with the Lord and won back the smile from Him. The Lord took Prahlad on His lap and blessed him. On Prahlad's entreaties He promised to forgive his father. He also reprimanded Brahma for giving 'asurs' such boons without thinking. It was like giving 'amrit' to a serpent.

Narayan then vanished. Thus it was that Jaya and Vijaya were freed from one birth of the three that they had to spend on this earth. The next birth of theirs was as Ravan and Kumbkaran who were killed by Vishnu in the form of Ram during the Treta Yug and the last one was as Shishipal and Dantavatra and Krishna in Dwapar killed the last two.

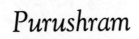

Purushram

Purushram

Purushram was born a Brahman but with the temperament of a warrior. He came into the world because by that time the Kshatriyas were holding sway as they were the acknowledged class who were the warriors and kings. They seem to have forgotten the respect due to the learned ones or the teachers — the Brahmans and the rishis. There seems to have been too much arrogance in the warrior class and they flaunted the rules of the Vedas in governing.

One such king was Kartarviryarjuna who ruled 'Hekaya' and was known for his strength and power. He was invincible. He even insulted Ravan who was camping on the river Narmada where Arjuna was bathing with his women. He was so strong that he was reputed to have one thousand arms and with them he blocked the river, which rose and wetted Ravan's tent. Ravan was very upset and angry but Kartarvirya captured him and made him the laughing stock of the women. He made Ravan a prisoner in his city of 'Mahishmati' and only released him after insulting him. This itself spoke badly of a ruling king in whose kingdom another king had come as a guest.

Then again while hunting in the forest he came to the Ashram of Jamadagni and the rishi entertained him and his entourage with the help of 'Kamadhenu', the divine cow. Kartarvirya became jealous of Jamadagni and asked his soldiers to steal the cow. The cow was taken crying piteously to the capital of Hekaya — Mahishmati. At that very time the youngest son of Jamadagni came to his father's

Ashram and on hearing of the stealing of the cow, he became extremely angry, he was Purushram — the sixth avtar of Vishnu who had come to clear the earth of the arrogant Kshatriyas. He fought Arjuna and his whole army and destroyed them. He killed Kartarviryarjuna whose one thousand sons ran away to their capital. Jamadagni was very upset at his son having killed an anointed king, who was supposed to be God for the people he ruled. Brahmin should not kill, but have the power of patience which makes him respected by all the people. He advised his son to go on a pilgrimage to the holy rivers and wash off the sin incurred by him. Ram obeyed his father and went (Purushram was also called Ram — Rama with the axe).

Ram had come back from his pilgrimage and was welcomed by his parents with great affection. Once Renuka his mother went to the river for water and saw the heavenly gandharva Chitrasen frolicking in the water with his apsaras and was quite taken in by his beauty. She stayed on longer watching the handsome man. She was late in coming home and when eventually she came, her husband who knew from his mind's eye as to what had delayed her got very angry and asked his four sons to kill her but they were hesitant and so he called out his youngest son Purushram to come and do so. Rama without a moment's hesitation killed his mother and his four brothers. The father was very pleased with him for obeying his command without hesitation and asked him to ask for anything he so desired. Ram asked him to bring them all back to life and erase the memory of his killing them from their memory forever. So it was, and everyone was happy.

The sons of Kartarvirya were seething with anger at their father's death — once when the four sons had gone to the forest, the sons of Arjuna came and killed Jamadagni as he was meditating. Renuka shouted in agony to Ram to come and help. Ram came running to the ashram and seeing what had happened just took his axe and putting it on his shoulder decided to teach all the Kshatriyas a lesson. He wanted to destroy all of them and went twenty-one times round the world and killed so many kings and their warriors that five lakes were filled with blood. He had come to remove evil that had crept in the system of good living and pious living and was an 'avtar' although the other Ram of Ayudhya was also alive and we have two avtars of Vishnu at the same time, but it is strangely also mentioned that Purushram will be one of the seven rishis in the next Manvantra.

After an argument with Laxman in Janak Court during Sita's Sawyamber when Ram broke the bow of Shiva-Purushram understood that Shri Ram was also the 'avtar' of Vishnu. He went away from there and threw his axe into the sea — Kerala is said to have risen from where the axe fell. Vishnu in the garb of Purushram had come to set the warrior class right and teach them how to behave as kings and warriors but He was an angry and hot-tempered 'incarnation' due probably because at the time when the kings and subjects did not quite know how to behave with each other. Society was very raw on this earth and force seems to have been the keyword to bring others to obey, but He gave way to 'Ram Avtar' to teach the people the correct way of behaviour in a peaceful and loving manner.

Vaman Avtar

Vaman Avtar

The guru of all the asurs is Sukre and he was at that particular time extremely fond of Mahabali, the then leader of the asurs. Bali was a very great and good king being the grandson of Bakt Prahlad and the son of Verlochan a great 'Giver'. Sukre had made Bali do the 'Visvajit Yagya' seeing how generous and kind his disciple was, and made Bali the most powerful King, no one could stand against him. He became the possessor of the greatest wealth in 'Bharat Varsh' and was loved by most of his people except the devtas led by Indra.

Although by having taken the *amrit* at the time of the churning of the ocean the devtas had become immortal, yet they could not withstand the strength and greatness of this 'asur' king, Bali who along with the other asurs was in great anger for being cheated out of the *amrit* and were keen to fight the devtas.

Mahabali had all the goodness and gave freely to all those who were in need, but he had a great fault and that was an over-riding desire to take the place of Indra in heaven and become the greatest in the three worlds. This desire smacked of arrogance and the ambition to oust an already entrenched king without reason of his rightful share — was not the right and lawful thing to do but he was very strong and could do what he wanted to.

The guru of the devtas Brashpati realised that devtas could not win against Bali who had decided to fight but the devtas did not wish to give their kingdom and therefore there ensued a great battle.

Brashpati advised the devtas to stop the fight and leave their kingdom and go into hiding as they could not win from Bali as his stars were very high at that time. Indra was first very upset and refused to leave his city of 'Amravati', but Brashpati persuaded him to do so and find some other way to destroy the asurs! The devtas obeyed and went into hiding as ordinary citizens of Mrityu Lok, but were extremely disturbed and upset at this state of affairs.

Balis' great desire to become Indra was fulfilled as he entered the capital of the devtas 'Amravati' and the threat of asur raj hung heavily in the three worlds with the fear that in the long run this will eventually bring disaster as the tendencies of the asurs were bound to come out even though Bali was generous and kind so far, in any case the balance of power was badly disturbed and the poor devtas were in a mess.

The devtas are the children of Aditi and Kashyap. Kashyap had been absent from his ashram for a very long time doing *tapasya* in the mountains. When he came back he found Aditi very distressed and asked her for the reason of her sorrow. Aditi told him about how the asurs had taken over the kingdom of her children and their King Bali had become invincible and her sons were roaming around rootlessly on earth. This she could not bear. Kashyap told her that if she prayed to Narayan for the first twelve days of *Phagan* and only drink milk during this time and repeat the *mantra* 'On Namo Bhagvate Vasudeva' Narayan will surely come to her and she could ask Him to deliver her children from their awful fate.

Aditi did just that and Narayan suddenly appeared on the tenth day, and told her that He knew her sorrow and although Bali was a very good and kind king, still he had become arrogant and must be taught a lesson as he could not take away other people's wealth and homes and make them destitutes. He promised to be born as her son, but she was not to tell anyone about it.

So it happened that she gave birth to a son who came in the full form of Narayan at birth, but soon changed into a tiny baby. As he grew older he still remained a tiny person looking more like a child. The child glowed with an ethereal light and the gods and devtas knew that this was Narayan himself. They gave him beautiful presents befitting an hermit, someone gave him an umbrella and someone a *kamandal* and another the sacred thread that he wore on his body, but he still remained very small and was named 'Vaman', his other name was 'Upendra'.

Mahabali decided to do a *yagya* as now he was the strongest of the kings in the three worlds. So on the holy grounds of 'Brighukachekha' on the northern banks of the river Narbada he started his yagna under the directions of his Guru Sukre. Soon the whole assembly saw a light coming from a distance and were very intrigued to see such a luminous person coming towards them. Bali got up and saw a very small boy with a *jata* on his head and an umbrella in one hand and a *kamandal* in the other, his whole body was shining like gold and everyone started to guess as to who this could be. They all got up as one man to welcome this celestial being. Bali looked towards him and in glowing words asked him to come and join in his *yagya*, and he washed the tiny feet and requested the young Brahman boy to ask for anything from him as was the right of a Brahman and he would give it there and then as was the *dharm* of a Kshatriya.

The tiny Vaman asked him for nothing more than the 'three paces of ground measured by his foot'. This was a surprise for Bali who told the young 'Vaman' that he could ask for much more as his tiny feet could measure very little. In the meantime Sukre guessed as to the identity of this tiny luminous figure and signalled to Bali not to give what was being asked for, but Bali had given his word and told his guru so, on which the guru got very angry and cursing Bali and left the 'yagnashala'.

Bali asked Vaman to proceed on measuring the ground with his foot. Soon Vaman rose to such a stature and took the full form of Narayan as 'Viraat Purush'. He was very awesome but Bali did not budge from his word and asked Him to do as was agreed upon. Narayan covered the entire earth with one step, the next He took the Devlok, Janaloka, Satyalok and Dyurloka. Brahma who was in Satya Lok was greatly excited as the gleam of the Lord's nails of the foot were soft like the moon-light. Brahma washed the foot with the water from his *kamandal* and the water that fell from the foot of Narayan flowed as a river named 'Mandakini' purifying all the spots it touched. On earth it became known as Ganga. Now Narayan asked Bali where was He to step for the third step, as all land had been taken by just this two steps. Bali quickly told him to step on his head as he was not afraid of going to the netherland pushed by Narayan Himself who had actually purified him by taking away his ego.

Narayan was very pleased with Bali who stopped his army from fighting the 'devtas'. They did not realise who Vaman was because when He took the 'Virat Roop' they had all fainted and only woke up when He had become 'Vaman' again. The Vishnu promised to look after Bali and his father and grandfather and keep them at 'Sutala' which He said "is dear to me and I shall keep guard over them and Bali would become Indra in 'Manvantra' known as 'Savarni' and all his asur tendencies will leave him and he will be a great Indra." And so came and went the Vaman avtar. The manifestation of life in the first human being.

Sri Ram and Sita

Sri Ram and Sita

society having evolved itself to the human form in this world of ours after the 'Vaman avtar', the Gods and devtas stopped guiding the inhabitants of this earth and mainly watched from their own 'Loks' the goings on in the realm of the human beings. This was then the coming of the second 'Yug' known as 'Treta' because three parts of goodness would remain in this world and one part of evil will slowly creep into the social order.

Society had to be made into a cohesive amalgamation of people where people settled down peacefully each taking his work seriously for the good of the whole. People had multiplied and as was seen during the time of Purushram — they started to behave arrogantly and had become without honour and dignity in their dealings with one another. Therefore someone had to rise above the self and teach the people their behaviour patterns in their different relationships with each other. So rose Ram as the seventh incarnation of Vishnu to set the standards of social order.

The story of Ram and his wife Sita is one of the most important 'Epic' in the Hindu Dharm written by Rishi Valmiki thousands of years ago and has been read and re-read everyday in different homes from the time it was written. It will be found in every Hindu household and the elderly will be reading it everyday, as a form of prayer before getting on with their chores. This 'Epic' gives a strange sense of deep satisfaction and peace and became extremely famous after

Tulsidas translated it into the vernacular language from Sanskrit in the Sixteenth Century AD.

It is the story of a king of Ayodhya who grew up to be a perfect human being and handed down the norms of behaviours to each and every aspect of human relationship, be it to his father, his mother, his brothers, his wife or to the subjects he ruled with love and duty. But those that did ill to others or behaved in an arrogant and disrespectable manner he stood up with strength and valour. Never afraid to fight wrong and uphold truth. He thus laid down rules for the correct behaviour of men and women to each other and made a disciplined and socially alert urban society each one knowing his duty to the other.

Ram along with his three other brothers was born to King Dashrath of Ayodhya in North India. King Dashrath did not have any children for a long time although he had three wives and after much prayer and *Yagya* he was blessed with Ram as the son of his eldest wife Kaushalya, the second wife Keykai was the mother of Bharat and Sumitra became the mother of Laxman and Shatrugan. The brothers grew up lovingly into a kingdom of prosperity and were taught the art of government and war by great rishis like Vishwamitra.

Laxman was very attached to Ram while Shatrugan was very fond of Bharat, but Ram was the ideal. He grew up to be a very graceful young man with long limbs and a body to match. He was extremely good looking although dark in complexion and was very well graced in his manners. He and Laxman were taken away by Rishi Vishwamitra to his hermitage when Ram was only 16 years of age — to kill some Rakshas that were troubling the rishis in their daily meditation and *havans*. These boys were young but the king could not refuse Rishi Vishwamitra as those that gave knowledge to the young and guided the kings in administering their kingdoms, were to be greatly respected and honoured. The boys went and killed the demon Subahu and drove Marich to the shores of the ocean — these were the Rakshas that troubled the saints. They guarded the ashram very well, Rishi Vishwamitra was able to complete his great 'Yagna' which had been polluted by the two rakshas.

He was very pleased with the boys and decided to take them to 'Mithla', the capital of Raja Janak's Kingdom of 'Vedeha' where Janak's daughter Sita was to have a Swayamvar and chose a husband for herself. Janak had the bow of Shiva with him and he proclaimed that whoever could string it would get his beautiful daughter Sita as his bride. Sita was very beautiful and lots of kings and princess had come to try their luck. None could even lift the bow which left Janak very sorry for setting such a standard and he lamented that his daughter would remain unmarried. Laxman could bear it no longer and decided to lift it and string it but Vishvamitra signalled to Ram to lift the bow as he was the elder. On trying to string it the bow broke with a resounding sound which brought Purushram the great bhakt of Shiva to the venue. He was very angry, but he soon realised that Vishnu had come in the form of Ram as he handed his own bow to Ram to string and Ram did so. He soon realised that Ram was a divine being and would also set the Kshyatriyas in order. From then on Purushram vanished.

Ram had been seen by Sita in the gardens of the temple of 'Gauri' where she had gone to pray and had asked Gauri to grant her such a one as her husband and that came true. So it was that she garlanded Ram and words were sent to Ayodhya about the Swayamvar and the king and all the three queens came for the marriage. Janak got the other three sons of Dashrath also married to his brothers' daughters and there was great rejoicing and the kingdom of Raja Dashrath was extremely happy.

Dashrath decided to give the throne to his eldest son and go into retirement, but his favourite wife Keykai had been given two rash promises when she saved his life in a battle field. Goaded by her maid, Keykai asked the king to make her son Bharat the king and send Ram into exile for fourteen years. Dashrath could not take back his word and with a bitter heart asked his eldest son as to what he should do. Ram without hesitation took leave of his father and his mother, as he believed in the Aryan theory of 'life can be dispensed with but not a word of honour'. Sita and Laxman were adamant on going along with him and so the three in garbs of hermits left the kingdom of Ayodhya and travelled towards the south, after taking the blessings of his parents and the subjects.

Bharat and Shatrugan had gone to their 'Nansaal' (mother family) when all this happened — on his return Bharat found his father dead and his elder brother exiled. He got very angry with his mother, and at once set out to bring Ram back. Nearly all the population of Ayodhya went with him and found Ram near the Ganges just about to cross the river to proceed into the forests of the South with the help of the chief of the boatmen Nishadraj. Ram refused to come back as he had given his word to his father. Bharat then took his wooden slippers and placed them on the throne of Ayodhya and himself settled in a hut on the outskirts of Ayodhya and lived in the same way as Ram and Laxman and Sita did in the jungle, wearing the clothes of a hermit and sleeping on kusha grass. He ruled from there in the name of his elder brother Ram.

Ram, Sita and Laxman made their way into the forests of Central India and stayed in a hut in the ashram of Agastha Rishi on the source of the river Godavari. Panchvati was the name given to their home where a sister of the great king Ravan of Sri Lanka came by chance. She fell in love with Ram and asked him to marry her. He sent her in jest to Laxman — saying that his brother would do so as he himself had his wife with him. Laxman got very annoyed with the woman and cut off her nose. This infuriated her and she went to her brother Ravan to seek his help. Ravan was livid with rage and as he had himself also gone for Sita's *Swayamvar* and could not lift the bow, he carried a great sense of humiliation at the hands of the young prince of Ayodhya and vowed to seek revenge.

Ravan was a very learned man and had the knowledge of ten heads, and is depicted with ten separate heads on his body but was an arrogant man having taken a lot of boons from Shiva and Brahma during his great *tapasyas*. These all went to his head and he became a demon or a *rakshas* even after gaining so much knowledge and in his desire to teach Ram and Sita a lesson he got Marich to become a golden deer. Seeing the deer Sita wanted Ram to bring his skin to decorate her home. Ram went after the golden deer which took him very far into the forest. Ram left Laxman to guard his wife and the hut, but as soon as the arrow hit the deer it shouted 'Laxman', 'Laxman' hearing which Sita got very worried and pestered Laxman to leave her and go to see what had happened to Ram. Laxman did not wish to go but she insisted. Therefore he drew a line with his bow and told her not to cross it come what may and went to look for Ram.

In the meantime Ravan dressed as a hermit came to Sita and asked her for alms. She got some fruit etc. from the hut to give it to him but she did not cross the line. Ravan insisted that he would only accept if she crossed the line as he would not take alms from a person who was bound in this way. Sita hesitated but soon stepped off the line and Ravan becoming himself grabbed her and putting her in his *Uran Khatola* (aeroplane) he flew towards Sri Lanka. Sita cried and cried, and took off her jewels and threw them on the earth. On the way they met a big bird 'Jatayu' who fought Ravan with all his might but was severely wounded and fell to the ground. Ravan then took Sita to his kingdom and put her in a garden retreat outside the town with lots of his women guards to guard her. He would come everyday and ask her to marry him but she refused. He could not take her by force as in that case he was cursed. His wife tried to persuade him not to take another's wife but he did not listen to anyone on this issue.

Ram and Laxman on finding out that they had been cheated came to their hut to find Sita gone and were absolutely distraught, and just set out to find her. They found the very injured 'Jatayu' who told them that Ravan had kidnapped her and taken her in his *Uran Khatola* to Sri Lanka. Jatayu died after that. Ram and Laxman then came across a tribe of monkeys hiding in the jungle under the leadership of Sugriv whose brother Bali had turned him out of his kingdom and also taken his wife as his own, though it seemed a misunderstanding. Bali thought that his younger brother wanted to take away his kingdom which rightly belonged to him as the elder brother but taking the wife of his brother was a crime which could not be condoned.

The Chief of Sugriv's army was Hanuman who became the greatest 'Bhakt' of Ram and stayed with him always after they met. This tribe had picked up the jewels of Sita from the jungle and showed them to Ram who asked Laxman to identify them, but since Laxman had only seen the feet of his sister-in-law he could only recognise the *payals* that Sita wore. The tribe of monkeys first made war on Bali and Ram killed him. Sugriv returned to his kingdom and got back his wife while Bali reached heaven because he had been killed by 'God' himself.

Now they formed a mighty army and reached the farthest end of Bharatvarsh and stood by the shore of the sea which divided Sri Lanka from the main land. Ram prayed to 'Shiva' and with the help of Nul and Neel who were blessed — that anything they touched would not sink — built a mighty bridge over the ocean of the stones touched by Nul and Neel, the stones did not sink into the ocean.

In the meantime Hanuman had been sent to Sri Lanka to inform Sita about Ram being very near and that she would be free soon. Hanumanji could fly being the son of the wind God 'Pavan', so flew into her garden resort and dropped the ring that Ram had given him for her to recognise him as his emissary. Hanumanji was very hungry by this time and wanted to eat some fruit from the garden. In the process he broke down many trees and plants and created great havoc. He was caught by Ravan's men and as a punishment his tail was tied with oiled clothes and set on fire. Hanumanji increased his tail to such an extent that the fire never reached his body. He jumped all over Sri Lanka burning most of the city of gold. Ram, Laxman and their army also reached there and a great war took place in which Laxman was injured and became unconscious but the main vaid of Ravan was brought from the city by Hanuman and he prescribed a herb *Sanjeevni booti* which grew only on a mountain of the Himalayas. Hanuman was dispatched and since he could not distinguish the herb, he brought the whole mountain to Sri Lanka. Laxman revived.

Ravan's brother Vibushan had been insulted by Ravan and he came over to Ram's camp and told him how to kill Ravan by shooting an arrow into his naval where 'Amrit' was stored and only when that was hit and become dry he could be killed. Kumbkaran a sleepy head of a brother of Ravan, and own son Megnath were all killed, alongwith Ravan. A great victory over evil was won.

Hanuman was sent to Ayodhya to inform about the victory and the return of Ram, Sita and Laxman and as the fourteen-year period was also over. Twenty days after 'Dessara' (the day of Victory) Ram returned to Ayodhya with his brother and wife in the *Pushpak Viman* (Ravan's aeroplane) and was crowned king. His rule was so good that even to this day people talk of 'Ram Rajya' as the ultimate aim. He listened to every aspect of every problem and even if it was very painful to him. Ram did as a king — he thought ought to do. He even sent Sita to the ashram of Valmiki when a *dhobi* was heard telling his wife that he would not keep her after she had lived in another man's house just like Ram had done. Sita stayed in Valmiki's ashram and had two sons born to her who became very bright and strong and highly intelligent and as young boys stopped their fathers' horse when Ram did the Ashvameda yagya to declare himself the highest king of the land. Ram did not marry again and while a wife must be with her husband at the time of the 'Yagna' he got a golden image of Sita made.

When Ram found his sons and wife, Sita did not return back to him but asked her mother earth to take her back and soon vanished into the earth. She had been found by Janak in a field while he was ploughing and was known as the daughter of the earth and was brought up as his own daughter. So ends one of the greatest 'Epic' of India.

Tulsidas Ramayan lays down the rules of conduct for each member of the family and society and this has had such an impact on the lives of people in India that Ram is acknowledged as the perfect human being and God incarnate.

Gandhiji always talked of "Ram Rajya", which he wanted for India.

Valmiki's Ramayan was written while Ram was alive, and Sita was staying in his ashram — which tells the story of Ram more as a human being — who took the Aryan rule into the South of India and was strict in maintaining discipline and did things that were right for him as a King, but not as a perfect human being, but due to the situation of that time, he had to get Sita to go through fire to prove her purity after living in Ravan's care. Later he sent her to Valmiki's ashram when a *dhobi* cast aspersions on her character. He seems to have treated her like a possession and not as a human being. He never married again and lived a life of a celebate although it was the custom to have more wives than one. His own father had married three and all wives were alive. The rishis advised Ram to do so when Ram did the Ashvamedic Yagya but he got a golden idol of Sita made to sit beside him at the yagna. He loved her beyond compare, but all through the Vedic period women have been treated as such (as said before) and so it fell into place to treat her as a commodity of the king.

Ram killed Bali from behind a tree because it suited him to have Sugreev on his side and by helping to win the kingdom of Bali he assured this tribal chieftain's loyalty and explained to Bali that he killed him surreptitiously because Bali had taken a lawfully wedded wife of Sugreev along with the Kingdom, which actually had belonged to Bali. Sugreev and Hanuman were on his side and it greatly helped him to overrule Southern India.

These two incidents stand apart and cannot be explained away except by accepting Ram as a human being who rose to great heights as a king according to the rules required at that time for the establishment of the rule of the Aryans, from north to the south of India, and he accepted the rules. In his private life also He accepted the rules as laid down by the accepted norms of that time. He rose mightly in the heart of people and became a true incarnation of Vishnu.

Later in the sixteenth century Tulsidas translated the Ramayan in his own style. He was absolutely taken up by the character of Ram and could see nothing wrong with him from the very beginning and cutting down a lot of Valmiki's work wrote the Ram Charit Manas in Hindi where none of the anger or laments shown by Ram as written down by Valmiki are mentioned and Ram is pure God from the beginning.

This 'Ram Charit Manas' is now so famous that Valmiki Ramayan is only read by the intellectuals and Tulsidas Ramayan is the one which is in everybody's heart and soul and has become the true story of Ram and Sita. People in the villages and the orthodox still carry the ancient norms and women remain uneducated and accept their plight as ordained by the Gods.

But Ram was a great king and laid the pattern of behaviour in a manner that society became a disciplined lot and seeing their king following the Vedic trends everyone tried to follow suit. Also he had won the whole of South India with its jungle tribes and brought them in the folds of the Aryans.

This 'epic' has found great favour in the whole of South East Asia and although the population in many countries has turned Muslim — they still remember and respect the story of Ram and Sita.

Balram and Krishna

Balram and Krishna

Vishnu is always accompanied by the serpent 'Adishesh' (on whose coil He rests) when He decides to take an 'Avtar' in the world. In the Treta Yug Adishesh came as the younger brother Laxman when Vishnu came as Ram to set right the standards of duty for society. Ram promised Laxman that in the dwaper Yug He shall be the younger brother and 'Adishesh' will be the known 'avtar' and will be known as Balram the man with the plough.

It stands to reason to have Balram with the plough to come and change the way of life of the people of this earth where humanity had multiplied and food got naturally from the forest, was running out. Someone had to find out ways and means to grow food by working at it. Balram was born to teach the people how to dig the earth and put in seeds and produce food in good quantity, and grow it where they wanted it thus making the settlements secure. Balram although holds the plough and is till today acknowledged as the eighth avtar, yet he is not much talked of nor the use of the plough stressed. His younger brother Krishna has slowly usurped his position and is more or less acknowledged as the 'Avtar'.

Krishna is not regarded as just an *Ansh* of Vishnu but Vishnu is full form with all the sixteen Kalas attributed to God. In no other avtar does Vishnu came in full form, therefore, Krishna is not counted as an 'Avtar' but the coming of God himself. Ram had fourteen Kalas but Krishna had sixteen, the extra two were trickery and corruption (*chhal* and *kapat*) which are also an essential part of the Almighty.

Krishna was born as the absolute image of Vishnu with four hands holding the four symbols but soon he became an ordinary baby thereby establishing himself as 'God incarnate'. He had come to kill his maternal uncle Kans who had wrought destruction and evil into the kingdom which he ruled. Kans was a very powerful king and had imprisoned his own father Ugarsen and usurped the throne. He was immensely disliked and everyone prayed for deliverance from him, hence Vishnu who had in some previous birth promised Deviki that he will be born as her son when the time came to spread light in the world, which would be in sore need of it. He came to Deviki — a cousin sister of Kans — and her husband Vasudev to rid the world of a vicious king and to give the message of the 'Bhagwat Gita' to the people who were to soon face the fourth and worst quarter of time 'Kal Yug'. The lesson of the Gita became an anchor for the people of this earth. No one can change the coming of the Yugs at their appointed time and the fourth quarter with very little good left in people, would require something for people to cling to for salvation.

Kans was told by the soothsayers that his cousin sister Deviki would be the one whose eighth child would destroy him. Narad Muni fanned the fire by showing Kans a eight-leafed lotus and told Kans that in a situation like this no one was sure which was the eighth child. Narad wanted Deviki to quickly have the eighth child and encouraged Kans to kill every child of hers, so that she did not waste time nursing one child after another and thus delaying the process of an early birth of the eighth child.

So it was that Kans imprisoned his cousin and her husband in his capital Mathura and killed each child as soon as it was born. But the seventh child was to be Adishesh in the form of Balram and had to be saved. Krishna asked a denizen of heaven named Jog Maya to come down to earth and remove the child from the womb of Deviki and take it to Gokul where one of the seven wives of Vasudev named Rohini was left in the care of Nand, a cowherd leader of that place and a great friend of Vasudev. Jog Maya was asked to put the baby in the womb of Rohini. Krishna made sure that everyone would go to sleep at the time this was being done. So it was that Balram was born to Rohini although conceived by Deviki. People were puzzled when it was discovered that Deviki was no more pregnant. Jog Maya was also asked to be born to Yashoda, the wife of Nand, and was to be exchanged with Krishna and it was she who flew out of the hands of Kans announcing the birth of his destroyer elsewhere. Krishna had told her that she would then be worshipped as Durga — Devyani — Ishani and in all the other names of the Goddess in various parts of the sub-continent.

It happened so that when Krishna was born on the dark Ashtmi of the month of 'Bhado' everyone guarding the prison went to sleep and the door opened by themselves and Vasudev took the baby across the river Yamuna to Gokul to the house of Nand and exchanged the baby Krishna with the daughter of his friend. Next day Kans heard of the baby's birth and came to kill it but Jog Maya flew into the sky as a streak of lightning and in a loud voice told Kans that his destroyer had been born and was safe on this earth.

Kans guessed that somehow the child at Nand's house was Deviki's son, but the people there aknowledged 'Him' as Nand and Yashodas' son. Kans tried his best to get him killed by sending a few rakshas, but each time Krishna killed the rakshas, without letting anyone know how it all happened and everyone was puzzled to find huge rakshasas lying dead in their town.

Krishna and Balram together played havoc amongst the local people by their pranks in collusion with all the little cowherds. Krishna played the flute so very well that the young women would leave off their work and run to the banks of the river Yamuna where he would be grazing his cows and playing his flute. As very young boys they would steal fresh butter from the churning pot of homes and when confronted deny having taken it! When Yashoda Maiyya asked him to open his mouth she would see the whole world in it and she would suddenly become conscious of the true identity of her son, but would soon forget it as was ordained by Krishna.

As the brothers grew up all the young women of the town would run up to where Krishna was playing the flute — leaving their chores unfinished and dance with the cowherds, thereby getting scolded by their mothers and mothers-in-law. Krishna developed a very deep attachment to a young married woman 'Radha' who became the true love of his life and a deep bond between them, which is till today sung in various songs. She became a part of his soul and has remained the one and only. Although he married several times later on and never did meet Radha after their youthful romance at Gokul-Brindaban and Barsana. The young people frolicked on the banks of the river and lived a life of abandon and happiness when Krishna was called to Mathura by Kans and fought an elephant and two wrestlers to show his power to the king and the people. He soon killed Kans and got his grandfather's brother Ugarsen out of prison and made him the king. He himself became the King of Dwarka and was aknowledged as the greatest of men of all times.

The great Mahabharat was fought between his cousins, the five sons of Krishna's father's sister Kunti and her husband — Pandu and their 100 cousins — the sons of Dhritrashtra. The story of the Great War between the 'Kauravs and Pandus' is the second great 'Epic' of India known as the Mahabharat. It is the tale of good winning over evil in the end where Krishna played a major role in advising both the parties to desist from this war — but sided with his cousins, the five Pandus. When His advice was not heeded by the Kauravas — With only his advice as his weapon — he taught Arjun the duty of a Kshatriya, telling him the true nature of life and death as Arjun refused to fight his own blood relations and his elders. He hung his head in shame in the battlefield of "Kurukshetra" where later the great battle of Mahabharat was fought to put down evil and bring back the rule of righteousness at the bidding of Krishna.

This semon to Arjun is the 'Bhagwat Gita', the crown jewel of all Hindu scriptures and is revered as the highest thought and philosophy of religion.

Gautam Buddha

Gautam Buddha

'Buddha' came to the earth as the ninth avtar of the Lord in 'Kalyug' to get the people away from rituals which had become extremely important due to the Brahman becoming very powerful. They found it to their advantage to let them remain so. They were in charge of keeping the people away from greed and materialism and had taken the place of the rishis and munnis of yora. They were supposed to guide the society into proper channels — but they themselves got involved in enriching themselves from the people by stressing the need for long and protracted rituals in Sanskrit which the common man did not understand and took a lot of wealth for it rather than the teachings of correct thought and behaviour. The Brahmans found that becoming rigid and sowing the seeds of superstition they could control the kings and the ordinary people. Therefore they made the 'caste system' very rigid indeed, and great grand rituals for prayers in homes and temples became the order of the day. The Brahmans became the mainstay of society and they took full advantage of it to enrich themselves and live a life of ease, vice and comfort. The true 'dharma' of the mind and soul was lost in fright of not doing the prolonged rituals as prescribed by the 'Pandits', who were the only ones that read the Vedas, etc., in Sanskrit and did not encourage anyone to go into deep study of the various 'Purans', etc. Truth became a haze.

So was born Siddartha to the Sakya Kings of Kapilavastu. Mahamaya his mother wanted the birth to take place in her own father's kingdom at Devadaha. The queen had a dream of a white elephant with six trunks entering her body before she became aware of this child in her body. The astrologers predicted that this child would be a great prophet or emperor and the king in great joy made all arrangements to send his pregnant wife to her father's house where she wanted to have the baby. The road between Kapilavatsu and Devadaha was made smooth and water vessels and banners and banana leaves put at different intervals. She went in a palanquin, but on the way at 'the Lubmni grove' she gave birh to a son, they say a spring appeared on its own and the child was bathed in it. But Mahamaya died seven days later and the child was brought up by his stepmother and an aunt named Mahapriyapati Gotami who fed him milk from her own breast. He is said to have been born in 507 BC.

Siddartha was brought upon great luxury and was married off at the age of sixteen to Yasodhara also known as Gopa or Bimba. A son was born to them when Siddartha was 20 years old and was named Rahul. But family life was not for Siddartha who also became known as Gautam. Once while going out with his charioter Chhauna and touring the city he saw an old man having been abandoned by his kith and kin. He saw another old man suffering from the agony of a disease and was told by Chhauna that that was the fate of all in the end. Then he saw a dead man being carried by his weeping relatives and the fourth incident that affected him was a mendicant who had given up the world and was searching for the 'Truth'! All this rackled in the mind of Gautama and even when a child was born to him he felt that he could not lead a life of luxury. They say that he left his wife and child sleeping and went with his charioter — but it is also mentioned in the Majjhema Nikaya that he renounced the world in front of his weeping mother and father and went into a world of the homeless.

He sat at the feet of Alara and Uderaka at Rajagriha now in Bihar and learnt the art of concentration of mind: neither consciousness nor non-consciousness. From there he went to Urvela and practised extreme penance and was reduced to a mere skeleton — but in spite of his great suffering he gained no enlightenment. He then started to keep away from sensual desire and food but to no avail. Thereafter he started to take food. One day he sat under a peepal tree at Gaya again in Bihar and vowed not to get up from there until he got that peace of mind for which he had been trying all his life. Although he had to face a lot of hardships he did not budge from his meditation. Ultimately after 19 years Gautama suddenly got his enlightenment and came to be known as the Buddha, the enlightened one. This happened when he was 35 years of age — after which he just wanted to teach the people the true way to "Nirvaan" or complete happiness.

After realising that 'Ahimsa' was the chief aspect for attaining peace he decided to preach what he had learnt after years of meditation. He travelled all over the country. He gave his first sermon at Somnath at Banaras. This was the "Dharma Chakra" Pravartana or the turning of the wheel of law. He travelled to his native land and his own son also became a monk. His teaching embraced all sects and castes and that there was no one high or low. He spoke in Pali which was easily understood by the common people who were fed up by the arrogant Brahmins who used to conduct their everlasting rituals in Sanskrit — which were hardly understood by the common man and as was the case of Purushram who killed the Kshatriyas because of their high-handed behaviour Buddha overcame the tyranny of the Brahmans.

But his teachings were all taken from the Hindu system and he lived and died as Hindu with a great thrust towards diminishing the rituals or prolonged worship of the many facets of the Hindu Gods. All was in the brain and in the words of wisdom that one thought and translated into action to all living beings — this then was the message taught by the Buddha who laid down the rules of behaviour thus:

His favourite sutra was the following Four Noble Truths — which exphasised the fact that life was full of pain — suffering due to desire — the removal of which would bring tranquility and peace.

(1) The first truth is the existence of review.
    All here is transient — sorrowful and full of pain.
(2) The second truth is the cause of sorrow. Desire is the cause of evils and hence it must be removed.
(3) The third truth is sorrow ceasing. Sorrow can be ended only by the elimination of desire. When sorrow ends — there is perfect bless. Life and death ends.

Buddha taught the eight-fold way namely: (1) right views, (2) right intentions, (3) right speech, (4) right action, (5) right living, (6) right effort, (7) right mindfulness, and (8) right concentration.

His guide on right living was:

(1) Let not one kill any living being
(2) Let one not take what is not given to him
(3) Let one not speak falsely
(4) Let one not drink intoxicating drinks
(5) Let one not be unchaste

According to Buddha a man should overcome anger by kindness, evil by good. Victory breeds hatred for the conquered who are unhappy. Never in the world hatred ceases by hatred, hatred ceases with love.

He discouraged questions as to what and wherefrom and where for — the world had come and good humouredly told a disciple that even Brahma would not know as to where He would go and from whence He came. A person should pay attention to this life and try to live a life of compassion — truth and renunciation.

He and his Bhikshu went each alone from house to house with their bowls and took what was given as food and never did ask for alms. They wore just one orange or yellow cloth and kept themselves submerged in study. Buddha taught that saintliness and contentment were to be found not in the knowledge of the Universe — in God — but in selfless and virtuous labour. He sent his disciples to all the lands to preach this gospel — telling them that the rich and the high are all one and that all castes unite in this religion as the rivers in the sea.

Buddism spread outside the shores of India in the South-East Asia — China, Indonesia, Burma, Tibet and Thailand but slowly lost its hold in its parent country where the original teachings of the Vedas and Puranas and the Upnishads came back. Still Buddhism holds a great attraction for the Hindu and Buddha has thus become the ninth incarnation. Buddha is accepted as a Hindu although his teachings became known as Buddhism. He founded many Sanghs which spread his teachings.

India has always thrown up a person required to balance the sea saw of life and accepts life as it is, tilting the balance to the required level of that time.

They say that perhaps idols of the other Hindu gods were made after Buddha whose disciples cut beautiful figures and heads of Him which the Hindus followed in relation to their own Gods.

Buddha left behind a lot of Sangha, and great and beautiful monasteries and universities were built for learning and concentration like Nalanda at Bihar and great scholars from abroad came to study there — they have left a lot of description of the great influence — Buddhism had a great influence on the kings that came after Gautam Buddha — like Ashoka who embraced Buddhism after the great battle and killings in Kalinga, what is now known as Orissa. Then Kaniska and Harsh all propagated this religion far and wide.

Buddha was a man of strong will and a great debater and put his opponent on the defensive. The teachings he taught were known as Hineyanism and later a lot of branches took off from these — like it happens in all religions and today Buddhism practised in different spheres differs to quite an extent from each other.

Buddha died at the age of 80 at Kushinagar identified with Kasia in Deoria is UP.

Kalki Avtar

Kalki Avtar

Kalki Avtar — which is the last of the Avtars of the 10 Avtars of Vishnu before Satyug again prevails on this earth — is still to come in the age we live in — Kalyug — when evil will become rampant. There will be salvation for only those that put their complete faith in the Almighty and do not go astray.

'Kalki' is reputed to come as a brave warrior on a white horse with a sword in His hand and shall destroy all evils. He will be fair of skin. He will come at the end of Kalyug. (Kalyug started on the midnight of 17th and 18th February 3102 BC). The duration of this Yug according to the European Calendar is 432,000 years of man.

Kalki being the incarnation of God will reveal His 'Life and Deeds' as and when He is born and as and how He choses to live. How He will bring about the great change from Kalyug to Satyug is completely in His hands.

Mother Goddess

Mother Goddess

According to the Bhagwat Puran the concept of the worship of the 'Mother Goddess' became prevalent in 'aryavarta' after Krishna asked Jog Maya — a denizen of the heaven to come in the form of the girl child of Yashodara the wife of Nand — a very close friend of Vasudev and be exchanged with Krishna who was to be born to Deviki, and had to be saved so as to kill Kans the demon King of Mathura. Also Jog Maya had transferred the foetus of the elder brother of Krishna to the womb of Rohini, one of the seven wives of Vasudev, who lived in Gokul under the protection of 'Nand'.

This emergence of 'Devi ma' as a separate identity to the three consorts of the holy Trinity 'Brahma, Vishnu and Mahesh' is as mentioned in the Bhagwat Puran and it seems very likely that the benevolent face of a female Goddess on her own took its stand only after Krishna's birth — before that the Goddesses were the Three Consorts, amongst whom Parvati became the main goddess and was very much worshipped by the women as the giver of boons in the shape of long life to their husbands on whom they wholly depended. Thereupon Parvati and Jog Maya became synonymous and the same names are given to both. Of course the Hindu understands that these are names given to the power of the almighty without which the aspects of the Unmanifest are static and impotent. The Hindu separated the power and gave it a female form because without the female — no one can be born or nourished and therefore she becomes the most powerful. She became 'Shakti'. The mother is the progenitor and as there is no real gender bias in the Hindu way of thinking, it is easily acceptable.

There are ancient references to female deities and many figurines are found depicting them. Mother earth was known as 'Bhoo-Devi' and was the original Goddess to the natives who lived in this sub-continent. But she became associated with agriculture and growing of food and became known as 'Shakambhari' — as vegetables and plants grew from her body.

The concept of the 'Mother Goddess' was used in tantrik ritual. This concept existed as far back as the stone age but the benevolent face of the mother Goddess seems to have come later. Durga, who was a fearsome deity, became soft and loving and was soon absorbed in Parvati — the eternal partner of Lord Shiva.

There are many other stories as to how the Devi was created. In one story she took form when from the filth of Vishnu's ears two demons took form while Vishnu was sleeping, they wanted to destroy Lord Brahma. Brahma sang the praise of Vishnu to wake Him from his slumber and get these pests killed. Brahma prayed to the 'Shakti' of Vishnu which took form as 'Bhagwati' and woke Him up to kill the two demons named 'Madhu and Kaitab'.

Another story is that once there was a great demon named Mahesha and he wanted to remove all the demi-Gods from their kingdoms and take over as the sole ruler of the three worlds. He succeeded in his nefarious designs and threw Indra — Agni — Vayu — Yam — Varun and the others out of their realms and they had to roam on 'Earth' without any power left in them. The demi-Gods then went to Brahma, Vishnu and Mahesh. The three Gods emitted — each a great brilliance from their mouths, which formed itself into a body and the great Goddess was born. The three Gods then gave her their weapons and the Goddess blocked all the paths by her thousand arms and Mahesha could not enter anywhere. The Goddess was on a lion and she destroyed the entire army of Mahesha-sur. She destroyed many others like Udagra, Valkala, Tamira, Chikshini, Chamar, Andhak, Atilam, Ugaamya, Ugraveerya, Mahakanu, Vidaalasya, Durdhas and Durmukhi. The human beings and Gods all praised the Goddess and asked her to come to their help whenever disaster struck them and she promised to do so.

Then there is the story of Shambhu and Nishambhu who wanted the earth dwellers to worship them and started to take away the portion reserved for the Gods during a 'yagna'. Soon they became so strong that they threw all the demi Gods from their seat in heaven. The demi Gods entreated the great rishis who advised them to pray to 'Durgama' as she had previously promised to come to their rescue whenever they were in trouble. She appeared on the banks of the Ganga. At that moment she was very beautiful. The servants of Shambhu and Nishambhu named Chanda and Munda saw her, and went to their Lords and Masters and described her beauty. The demons both wanted her brought to them and ordered Chanda and Munda to get her. Kali declared that she had taken a vow that only if anyone could get the better of her in battle she would be his. Sugreev, another of the henchmen of Shambhu and Nishambhu, told her about the fate of all the demi Gods at the hands of the demons but she refused to break her pledge. The two demons were very angry and sent another demon named Dhoomirlochan to bring her to them by force. The Devi came into her own and tore up the entire army of the demons with the help of her lion. Another army was sent to surround the Himalayas where she was stationed, the Goddess got mad with rage and from her forehead appeared a jet black form which was the other form of Durga — Kali and she destroyed every demon. On her destroying Chanda and Munda she became known as 'Chamunda'.

As Kali when the Goddess destroyed Shambhu and Nishambhu she became overjoyed and started her dance of death wearing a garland of skulls and having all the weapons in her hands and even though the demi Gods prayed to her to stop. She would not, then Lord Shiva threw himself on the bodies of the dead demons, whereas Kali Parvati saw that she was nearly dancing on her husband's body — she took out her tongue in great anguish and surprise and stopped her 'Tandav'. Her tongue was red in colour and that is the image of Kali accepted by her worshippers especially in the eastern parts of India. In most parts of the North Mother Goddess is worshipped as 'Durga' on her vehicle the lion. She has four, eight or ten hands. One hand is always raised in a blessing.

Still Shambhu and Nishambhu did not heed the warnings of Lord Shiva and Lord Kartikeya who headed the army of the demi-Gods. There began a great battle. A demon named Raktabeeja began to fight with great force and each drop of blood that fell from his body became another demon. The Goddess in her Chamunda form swallowed Raktabeeja. Then came Shambhu and Nishambhu but the Goddess declared that she was the 'Ultimate Form' and all beings shall go into her at the time of *Pralaya* — hence she cannot be killed by anyone and soon she killed the two demons. She took nine forms in the whole battle, but promised all the demi-Gods and the earth kings that she will come to them whenever they wanted her and thus she did in the form of Durga.

Durga got her names from destroying a demon named Durg. Shiva asked his consort Parvati to do the needful and she accepted and assumed a thousand arms with a number of weapons in them. The demon made himself into buffalo and there was a long battle in which she killed the demon with her trident and the Gods gave her the name Durga.

The names of the Goddess which springs from the fountainhead Parvati are numerous as she takes different forms and is called by a different names each time.

She is Parvati in her child form — Uma — the beauty known as Gauri-Hemavati — daughter of the Himalayas, Jagat Mata — Bhawani — the Goddess of the Universe. In her terrible form — she is Durga — the inaccessible Kali or

Shyama — the dark complexioned one. Chandika or Chandi — the fearful one — Kapila — Bhairavi — the terrible. Ishani — the Consort of Shiva (Ishan). Tara as Bhuvanshvari —Tarini — Dhumavati — Chhinmasta — Shodashi complete with all her sixteen Kalas. Bahala — Kamala — Matangi is another name given to her as Shakti — Chandi she is also called — but she is the Mahadevi or 'Durga'.

Temples of the mother Goddess are now in every hills side on the Himalayas and Vaishnav Devi has become a very sought after pilgrimage spot. Jwalamukhi is in Himachal Pradesh. Kheer Bhawani is in Jammu and Kashmir. In the south the most famous are the Meenakshi temple in Madurai, Tamil Nadu and Kanya Kumari at the land's end at Cape Comorin in the southernmost end of India. All over in every city and village there are temples. In Rajasthan there is Jagat Mata temple in Udaipur. In UP near Allahabad there is a Tantrik temple known as Vindhya Wasini Devi temple. In Amritsar, Punjab, there is the Durgiani temple. Dakshveshwar is a Kali temple at Calcutta and so is the Kalighat temple at Calcutta. Every place has a new name for the Goddess and no other power of Gods has so many.

All the Gods pray to the Goddess and the demi-Gods ever wanting her protection. She was worshipped by Ram before he took on Ravan in the great battle at Sri Lanka and the Pandavs prayed to her whenever they found themselves in difficulty.

Special nine days are set aside for 'Durga Puja' twice a year and are known as the 'Navratra', the main being celebrated in the month of Ashwin (September-October) when huge pandals are decorated in community centres. Especially in Bengal puja is done with great pomp and show. Most households in India celebrate this in their homes just the nine days before Dessara. The other 'Navratri' is in Chait (March-April). This one is more or less a private homely affair.

The Goddess alongwith Hanumanji and Ganeshji have become the most worshipped deities of today. They bestow boons and remove obstacles. The Holy Trinity looks on benevolently.

Arti

The Arti is a ceremony performed in adoration of a deity by circular movement of a lighted lamp before "Its" image — at the end of a 'Puja'. It is generally accompanied by singing of a prayer to that deity which is also known as an Arti.

The Hindus treat their 'Gods' like themselves and bestow upon them all that they would like to bestow upon themselves. Homes usually have a corner — an almirah or a small room — set apart for a little *mandir* (temple) where the favourite deity or deities are kept and where one or more members meditate — do their *Jaaps* or read their scriptures everyday or whenever they desire to do so.

The elder of the family having reached the 'Vanprasth' stage has the time and the inclination to devote to the *mandir*. He or she cleans it every day after a bath and is seen chanting some Sanskrit shlokas or reading the scripture for a considerable time in the morning and sometimes in the evenings also. After which the Arti is performed, usually 'Om Jai Jagdish Hare' addressed to the 'One Supreme Lord' is sung, but if it is a puja to a particular deity, due to it being a festival of that deity, or that particular deity is the favourite of the one doing the puja, then the 'Arti' sung is particular to that deity.

There are festivals attributed to different important deities all through the year and the temples and individual homes celebrate them with great enthusiasm. The pujas at home are always finished with everyone standing up and singing the 'Arti' to that particular 'Deity' whose festival it is and everyone taking the 'arti lamp' turn by turn and circling it before the image.

The temples of the town do so with throngs of people attending and while everyone sings, only the priest holds the 'Arti' and does the movement. The 'Arti' is performed twice a day in a temple — once in the morning after the deity has been woken up, bathed and fed, then at the time of sunset when the evening chores are over. These times are very beautiful as the deity or deities are dressed in the most fabulous clothes, especially during a festival. Everyone joins in the singing. The 'Arti lamp' in a temple has many wicks lighted while in a home just one wick or five-wicks are the norm. The mould of the 'Arti' is a special one with a handle attached to the sockets made for the wicks and oil, and can be of any metal. It is available in all shops selling 'Puja items'. But just a wick in a 'Katori' (a small deep vessel) placed in a metal plate can serve the purpose.

Afterwards the lamp of the arti is taken around to those present and they take the flame symbolically with both their hands and touch it to their faces. Offering of money is put in the plate which carries the lighted lamp. This is done both at home and at the temples.

The words of the songs sung are pure adoration of the deity describing in superlative terms, the physical glory and temperaments and the clothes and jewels that are always worn by 'It', the symbols are also described. The singer in the end asks the deity to bless and accept him or her in 'Its' grace and show him the path to righteousness and truth and to grant him his needs in this world and salvation after death.

Arti is also done to human beings in rare cases as a form of welcome or when they are going to a "war" or a far off land to keep them safe. This is usually known as "Arta". No money is put in the plate which carries the lamp at such times except during a wedding.

I am writing down the Artis that are for the main Gods and Devtas, and are sung generally at the temples and at home.

Om Jai Jagdish Hare

Om jai Jagdish hare, swami jai Jagdish hare
Bhakt jano ke sankat chhin mein dur kare
Om jai Jagdish hare...

Joe dhyave phal paave dukh vinshe manka
Swami duk bin se manka
Sukh sampati ghar aave kasht mitei tan ka
Om jai Jagdish hare...

Maat pita tum mere sharan gahun kiski
Tum bin aur na duja aas karun jiski
Om jai Jagdish hare...

Tum puran paramatma tum antar yaami
Swami tum antar yaami
Paar Brahma Parmeshwar tum sab ke swami
Om jai Jagdish hare...

Tum karuna ke sagar tum palan karta
Mein murakh khal kami kripa karo bharta
Om jai Jagdish hare...

Tum ho ek agochar sub ke pran pati
Kis vidhi miloon daya mein tum ko mein kumati
Om jai Jagdish hare...

Deen bandhu dukh harta thakur tum mere
Apne haath uthao dwar parha (parhi) tere
Om jai Jagdish hare...

Vishya vikar metao paap haro deva
Shradha bhakti barhao santan ki sewa
Om jai Jagdish hare...

Tan man dhan sub kuch ha tere 'Prabhu'
Tera tugh ko arpan kya laage mera
Om jai Jagdish hare...

Om Jai Jagdish Hare

Om — Victory to Hare, the Lord of the Universe
One who removes the troubles of His devotees in a minute,
He who meditates upon Him gets his desires fulfilled
And the sorrow of the heart and mind is destroyed.

Contentment and wealth enter his house
And the afflictions of the body are destroyed
You are my mother and my father where else
        would I take refuge
There is no other on whom I can depend and look for hope

You are the Supreme soul — You know every thing that is
        in one's mind and heart
You are the perfect God, the most powerful God and
        the Lord of everyone

You are the Ocean of compassion — You are the protector
I am a stupid — wicked and lustful being, be kind and
        compassionate to me, O'sustainer

You are the remover of miseries and are the Lord of life
How do I meet you, O'Lord! I beseech you

You are the helper and remover of pain and suffering
    You are my God,
I have come to your door please raise your hands
    to help me

O' Lord! wipe away the material attachment
    and remove my sins,
Increase my faith and devotion and let me
    serve the saints

Everything — my body, my mind and heart — and my wealth
    is all yours My Lord
I offer it back to you, as it
    does not really belong to me.

Ganesh ji ki Arti

Jai Ganesh, jai Ganesh, jai Ganesh deva
Mata jaaki Parvati pita Mahadeva
Laddun ke bhog lagen sant kare sewa (Jai)

Eik dant dayavant, chaar bhuja dhaari,
Mustak sindoor sohe musa ki sawaari (Jai)

Andhan ko aankh dete kodhin to kaaya,
Baanjhan ko putra dhey nirdhan ko maya (Jai)

Haar chadhey pushp chadhey aur chadhey meva
Sub kaam purna karo Sri Ganesh deva (Jai)

Jai Ganesh, jai Ganesh, jai Ganesh deva,
Vighn vinashik swami sukh sampati deva

Parvati ke putra kahave Shankar sut swami
Gajanand, Gannayak bhaktan ke swami (Jai)

Ridhi Sidhi ke maalik mooshak asawari
Kar jodhey binti karte anand ur bhaari (Jai)

Pratham aap ko pujat shubh mangal data
Sidh hoye sub kaaraj daridra hut jaata (Jai)

Sund-sundla ind inthala mustak par chand
Karaj sidh karavo Kaato sub phanda (Jai)

Ganpatiji ki arti jo koi nar gaave
Tub Baikunth param path nischai hi paava (Jai)

Ganesh ji ki Arti

Victory to Ganesh, victory to Ganesh, victory to
     Ganesh deva
Your mother is Parvati and father is Mahadeva,
Laddoos are offered to you as Prasad, great saints serve upon
     you.
You have one tooth, you the giver of good and have four
     arms
The forehead is decorated with Sindoor and the mouse is
     your vehicle.
Blind get eyes from you and you give body to the lepers
You give sons to barren women, the poor you give wealth,
You are offered garlands and flowers and dry fruits
All tasks are well taken care of by you Sri Ganesh deva
     Victory to Ganesh, victory to Ganesh, victory to
     Ganesh deva
     Destroyer of obstacles, you give happiness and wealth
You are known as the son of Parvati and Shiva,
Elephant faced and leader of all the devotees,
Husband of Riddhi and Siddhi you ride a mouse,
With folded hands we pray to you and derive great
     happiness,
You are the one that people pray to, O' the giver of welfare,
All tasks are successfully accomplished and poverty is
     banished,
You have a trunk on your face and the moon on forehead
Give success to all my tasks and ventures and remove all
     that binds me,
Who ever sings the arti of Ganpatiji
Will definitely reach the highest place in heaven.

Shiv ji ki Arti

Jai Shiv Omkara, har Shiv Omkara
Brahma Vishnu sadashiv urdhangni dhara (Jai))

Ekaanan chaturaanan panchanan raje
Hasaanan garudhaasan Vrishvahan saaje (Jai)

Do bhuj chaar chaturbhuj dus bhuj tei sohey
Teeno roop nirakhata tribhuvan jun mohey (Jai)

Akshmala banmala mundmala dhari
Chandan mrigmad sohey bhaaley shashidhari (Jai)

Shwetambar pitamber baghambar
Sankadik brahmadhik bhutadik sange (Jai)

Kar me shresht kamandalu chakra trishul dharta
Jagkarta jagharta jagpaalan karta (Jai)

Brahma Vishnu Sadashiv jaanat aviveka
Pranvaakshar ke madhya ye teeno eka (Jai)

Trigun Shiv ki arti joi koi nar gaave
Kahat Shiwanand swami munvaanchit phal paave (Jai)

Shiv ji ki Arti

Victory to Shiv the Onkar you are the primeval
    sound of Onkar
Brahma Vishnu and the eternal Shiva from whose head flows
    the Ganga

One faced (Vishnu), four faced (Brahma), five faced (Shiva)
    shine
So do the Swan (the vehicle of Brahma), Garuda (the vehicle
    of Vishnu, and the bull (the vehicle of Shiva) shine

Eight arms (Brahma), four arms (Vishnu), ten arms (Shiva)
    beautify you
Seeing the three forms, the people of the three world
    are bewildered

Garlands of beads (Brahma), garland of flowers (Vishnu),
    garland of skulls (Shiva), Sandal (Brahma), saffron
    (Vishnu) and the moon (Shiva) on the forehead pleases,
They wear white clothes (Brahma), yellow clothes (Vishnu)
    and a lion cloth (Shiva)

They keep the company of Sankadik Brahmadik and the
    ghosts
In their hand is the Kamandal (Brahma), disc (Vishnu)
    and the trident (Shiva)

They are the creator, the destroyer and the preserver of
    the Universe,
The uninitiated know Brahma, Vishnu and the eternal
    Shiva to be different
But the syllable 'OM' they are one
Who so ever sings the Arti of Shiva, of three qualities
attains the desired fruit, so says Shivanand Swami.

Sri Ram Chandra ji ki Arti

Sri Ram Chandra kripaala bhaj mun haran bhavbhas
  darunam
Nav kanj lochan kanj mukh kar kanj pad kanjaarunam.

Kandarpu agnit amit chavi nav neel neeraj sundrum,
Patpeet maanu tarhit ruchi shuchi naumi janak sutavarum.

Bhaju din bandhu dinesh daanav daitya vansh nikandanum,
Raghunand anand kand kaushal chand Dashrath nandnum.

Sir mukut kundal tilk charu udaar ang vibhushnam,
Aujanu bhuj sar chaap dhar sangram kit kar dushnam.

Iti vadti Tulsidas Shankar shesh muniman ranjanum.
Mum hriday kanj nivaas karun kamaadi khaldal ganjanum

Mum jaahi raanchiyo milhi so ver sahaj sunder saanvro,
Karuna nidhaan sujaan sheel sneh jaanat raavroo.

Eehi bhaanti gauri ashish sun siye sahit hiye harshit ali,
Tulsi Bhavani puji puni puni mudit man mandir chali.

Jaani gauri anukool Siya hiya harsh na jaat kahi,
Manjul mangal mool, baam ang pharkan lagey.

Sri Ram Chandra ji ki Arti

O! heart and mind, remember and repeat the name of Ram,
Who removes the dreaded fear of the material world,
Has eyes like newly blossoming lotus,
and face and hand and feet are red like a new born lotus.

His beauty is equal to countless cupids,
His body is dark like the new blue rain clouds full of water.

His yellow clothes shining like lightening amid those clouds,
I bow to you Sri Ram — the husband of Sita, the favourite
daughter of Janak.

The companion and kin of the poet shining like the sun,
He uproot the hordes of demons and bring joy to the family
of Raghu.

The son of the house of Raghu and the son of Kaushalaya
and Dashrath,
He is the source of great happiness and joy.

With a crown on His head, earings in His ears, an auspicious
mark on the forehead,
Beautiful jewels on different parts of His body,
His long arms reaching up to His knees, holding a bow and
arrow,
He has won Khar and Dushnam in battle.

He delights the heart of Shiva, Tulsidas and the sages and
destroys the enemies like desire, anger and greed,
May He, who is like a pure lotus reside always in my heart.

Sri Krishan ji ki Arti

Arti kunj behari ki, Girdhar Krishan murari ki

Gale main Vyajantimala bajawe, murli madhur bala,
Shravan mein kundal jhal kala, Nand ke anand nandlala,
Nainan beech basi ur beech, suratiya roop ujaari ki,
Girdhar Krishan murari ki, Arti kunj behari ki.

Kankamay mor mukut vilsey, Devta darshan ko tarse.
Gagan say suman bahut barsay, Bajat moohn chang aur
    miridang,
Gvalene sung, Laaj rakh gop kumari ki,
Girdhar Krishan murari ki. Arti kunj behari ki,

Jahan te pragat bhai Ganga. Kalush kali harni Sri Ganga,
Dhari Shiv sheesh jata ke beech Radhika gaur
Shyam patchare ki, chavi nirkhe banwari ki,
Girdhar Krishan murari ki. Arti kunj behari ki.

Chahoon dishi gopgwal dhenu, Baaj rahi Yamuna tat benu,
Hansat mukh mund varad sukh kand Vrindavan.
Chand ter suni leyu deen bhikari ki,
Arti kunj behari ki.

Sri Krishen ji ki Arti

We sing and perform the arti of (Kunj behari), one who roams
in the groves and is known as (Girdhar), one who holds
the mountain, (Krishan murari) and who is the enemy of Mura
    the demon.

The one who wears a Vyajanti garland on his neck
and plays the flute so melodiously.

In His ears he wears black earings and is the
darling and the source of delight to Nand
whose son He is known as.
His beautiful face stays in the heart,
We sing the arti of the one who held the mountain
The one who is the enemy of 'Mura'
The one who roams in the groves and gardens.

His crown is gold with peacock feathers and looks lovely
The Gods crave for a glimpse of Him
Flowers in profusion shower from the sky
as He dances with the milk maids
with drums and chambells sounding sweet music
We sing the arti of...

O' Krishna you are the one who protects
the modesty of the cowherd and the milk maids,
We sing the arti of Krishna who roams in
the groves and garden and held the mountain
and is the enemy of 'Mura' the demon.

From whom manifests the Ganga, the
remover of all sins and impurities of Kalyug,
Shiv caught its fall in between the locks of his long hair,
Radhika is fair and Krishna is dark yet we love the form of
    Krishna.

We sing the arti of Krishna the one who roams in
the groves and gardens and hold the mountain and
    is the enemy of 'Mura'.
The cowheads and cows are all around him
as He plays the flute on the banks of the river Yamuna
With a smile on his lips He is the source of ecstasy
and giver of boons, He, who lives in Vrindavan
O' Krishna! Listen to a beggar's small prayer
We sing the arti of Krishna who roams in the groves
and garden and lifts a mountain and is the enemy of 'Mura'.

Saraswati ji ki Arti

Arti kijaa Saraswati ki
Janan vidya buddhi bhakti ki
Jaaki kripa kumati mit jaaye
Sumeran karat sumati gati aaye
Shuk Sankadik jaasu gun gaaye
Vani roop anadi shakti ki (Arti...)

Naam japat bram chutei jiye ka
Divya drishti shishu udhar hiye ki
Milhi darash pawan siye piya ka
Uraayee surbhi yug yug kirti ki. (Arti...)

Rachit jassu bal ved puraan
Jate granth rachit jagnana
Taalu chchand swer mishrit gaana
Jo aadhar kavi yeti sati ki (Arti...)

Saraswati ki, veena vani kala janani ki,
Arti kije Saraswati ki.

Saraswati ji ki Arti

Perform the arti of Saraswati,
The Goddess of knowledge, of creation,
        intellect and devotion,
By whose grace the baseness and perversity in the intellect
        is destroyed,
Remembering whom, one gets wisdom and salvation.

Suka and Sankadik and the others sing her praise
Being the speech incarnate of the 'Prime force'
Perform the arti of Saraswati of knowledge of
creation — intellect and devotion,

Repeating whose name all doubts that lie in the
heart and mind are destroyed.

The divine light comes into the mind of a child
One even gets to see Ram the husband of Sita
The fragrance of His fame spreads through all the Yugs
Perform the arti...

By whose power the Vedas and the Purans were created
Stanzas were created with rhythm, metre, sound and song
The very basic — the source of poets — ascetics and women

Perform the arti...
The sonorous sound of Saraswati's Veena
Is the birth of all arts and creation
Perform the arti...

Laxmi ji ki Arti

Om jai Laxmi mata, maiya jai Laxmi mata
Tum ko nishden sewat Har Vishnu vidhata

Uma Rama Brahamani tum hi jagmata
Surya chandrama dheyawat Narad rishi gaata

Durga roop niranjani, sukh sampati data
Jo koi tum ko dhayata ridhi sidhi paata

Tum paatal niversini, tum hi shubh data
Karm prabhav-prakashini bhav nidhi ki traata

Jis ghar main tum rahitin sub sadguna aata
Sub sumbhav ho jata, mun nahin ghabrata

Tum bin yagya nahin hovei, vastra na koi paata
Khan-paan ka vaibhaw, sub tum se aata

Shubhgunh mandir sunder, shrirodhi jaata
Rattan chatur darshan tum bin kohi nahi paata

Maha Laxmi ji ki arti jo koi nar gaata
Ur anand samata, paap uttar jaata

Sthir char jagat bachave shubh karm nar laata
Ram pratap maiya ki shubh drishti chahata

Laxmi ji ki Arti

Om — victory to mother Laxmi — mother victory to mother
   Laxmi
Brahma, Vishnu and Shiva serve you night and day
You are Uma — Rama Brahmani
You are the mother of the Universe
The sun and moon meditate upon you
The sage Narad sings your praise.
You are the transcendental Durga
giver of happiness and wealth
Whoever meditates upon you
attains wealth and prosperity.
You reside in the nether land (Patal lok)
You give auspiciousness to your devotees
You illuminate the influence of action
You are the protector of the wealth of the Universe
In which ever house you reside every thing becomes possible
The mind stays unperturbed
No sacrifice (Yagya) can be performed without you
No one gets clothes without your sanction
The glory of food and water is because of you
You are beautiful, the abode of noble virtues
and born of the milky Ocean
No one can attain the four gems without your blessings
Whoever sings the arti of Mahalaxmi
Has the heart filled with joy
And all the sins are destroyed
The moving and stationary world
are saved by you
You sow the seeds of good deeds in human beings
Ram Pratap — O' Mother, seeks your benign look
and blessings.

Parvati ji ki Arti

Jai Parvati mata jai Parvati mata,
Brahma sanatan devi shubh phal ki daata. (Jai)

Arikul padm Vinashini jai sewak trata
Jag jeevan Jagdamba Harihar gun gaata. (Jai)

Suih ko vahan saaje Kundal hai saatha
Dev Vadhur jag gavat nritya karat ta tha. (Jai)

Satgun roopsheel atisunder naam sati kahlata
Himanchal ghar janami sakhiyan rangraata. (Jai)

Shumb Nishumbh vidare Himanchal syata
Sahastre bhuj tanu dharike chakra liyo haatha. (Jai)

Srishti roop tu hi hai janani Shiv sung rangraata
Nandi bhragi been lahi saara madmata. (Jai)

Devan araj karat hum chit ko lata
Gaavat de de taali mun main rang raata. (Jai)

Sri Pratap arti maiya ki jo koi gaata
Sada sukhi nit rahata sukh sampati paata. (Jai)

Parvati ji ki Arti

Victory to Parvati mother — victory to Parvati mother
The eternal Goddess and giver of all auspicious fruit
Victory to the Goddess, the destroyer of enemies and
    protector of attendants.

You are the life of the Universe — Hari and Shiv
    sing your praise
Your vehicle, the lion, looks beautiful alongwith your earing
    in your ears,
Celestial women sing and dance in your honour,
You were born as Sati during Satyug — a beautiful woman
    born in the house of Himanchal, you played around
    with your girl friends
You killed the demon Shumbh and Nishumbh in the
kingdom of Himanchal
Assuming one thousand arms and holding a disc in one hand
You alone are the form of creation, O'! giver of life, enjoying
    the company of Shiva,
All the attendants — Nandi and Bhringi are full of joy,
We pray to you O Goddess whom the Gods themselves
    serve with clapping of hands we sing your praise and
    joy fills our hearts and soul
Those that sing the arti to you — mother
will always remain happy and wealthy

Sri Durga ji ki Arti

Jai Ambe Gauri maiya jai Shyama Gauri
Tum ko nishdin dhyawain Har Brahma Shivji

Maang Sindoor birajat teeka mrigmud ko
Ujwal say doe naina chandra badauni ko

Kanak saman kalever raktambar raaje
Rakt pushp gal mala kanthan par saaje

Kehari vahan raajat kharak khapardhari
Sur nar munnijun sewat tin ke dukh haari

Kanan kundal shobhit nasagre moti
Kotik chandra devakar sum raajat jyoti

Shumbh Nishumbh bidaare Mahisha sur ghati
Droom vilochan naina nishdin madmati

Chand Mund sanhare shonit beej hare
Madhu Kaitabh doi mare sur bhaye heen kare

Brahmani Rudrani tum Kamla rani
Aagum nigum bakhani tum Shiv patrani

Chausath yogini mangal gaavat nritya karat bhairon
Bajat taal mridanga aur baajat dumru

Tum hi jag ki mata tum hi ho bharta
Bhagtan ke dukh harta, sukh sampati karta

Bhuja chaar ati shobhit kharag khapardhari
Mun vanchit phal pavat sevat nar nari

Kanchan thaal birajat agar kapur bati
Srimalketu main rajat koti rattan jyoti

Ma Ambeji ki arti jo koi nar gaave
Kahat Shivanand swami sukh sampati paave

Sri Durga ji ki Arti

Victory — O' mother Durga — the fair one and victory to
    you the dark one.
Hari-Brahma and Shiv meditate upon you everyday
The parting of your hair is filled with sindoor and a auspicious
    mark of deer musk is on your forehead,
Two bright eyes shine in your moonlike face.
Your body is like moon light. You wear red clothes.
Red is the garland round your neck looking beautiful
Riding a tiger as your vehicle you look gorgeous with a
    sword and a begging bowl in your hands
The Gods, saints and sages serve you, whose distress you
    remove.
The earings in your ears look lovely and you have a bead
    on the tip of your nose
Your lustre shines like crores of moons and suns
You killed Shumbh and Nishumbha, the bull faced demons
    and you killed Dhumra Valochan
You killed Chand and Mund and Rakta beej
You killed Madhu and Kaitabh and made the Gods fearless
You are Saraswati, you are Parvati and you are Laxmi
You expound the Vedas and their auxiliaries
    and you are the chief queen of Shiva
Sixty-four yogines sing your praise
    and Bhairon goes into a ecstatic dance
    with the rhythmic sound of mridung and dumru
    (kind of drums).

You are the mother of the Universe and
    you alone are the sustainer,
You take away the suffering of your devotees
    and give contentment and riches to them
You dazzle with your four arms holding
    the sword and the begging bowl in them
Those that serve you will get their hearts desire
A golden plate with incenses, camphor and wick
    is placed before you
You reside in your splendour in Malketu
Who ever sings the Arti of Durga Ma (Ambe)
    will get contentment and wealth — so says Swami
    Sivanand.

Sri Kali Mata ki Arti

Ambe tu hai Jagdambe Kali, jai Durge khaparwali
Tera hi gun gaave Bharati,

O' Om maiya hum sub utaren teri arti
tere bhakt jano par mata bheer hai parhi bhari
Daanav dal par toot paro ma karke sinh savari
Sau sau singhon se hai balshalli hai dus bhujahon waali
dukhiyon ke dukh nivaarti
Om maiya hum sub utarein...

Ma bete ka hai is jag main bara hi nirmal naata
Poot kapoot sunne hain par na mata sunni kumata
Sub pe karuna darshaane wali Amrit barsaane wali
     dukhiyon ke dukhre nivaarti
Om maiya hum sub utarein...

Nahin maangte dhan daulat, na chandi, na sona
Hum to maange ma tere mun main aik chota sa kona
Sub ki bigri banane wali laaj bachane wali
Satiyon ke sat ko sanvarti
Om maiya hum sub utareni teri arti

Sri Kali Mata ki Arti

O' mother dark and invincible — you are the mother
of the Universe — the other face of Durga with the sword,
The ones' who live in 'Bharat' sing your praise

Mother we perform your arti
O' mother great calamity has befallen on your devotees
come and destroy the demons, with your ten arms, riding
     on your tiger

You with your ten arms are stronger than hundreds of lions
You are the remover of the woes of the distressed
O' mother dark and invincible...

The relationship of a mother and son is very pure
Unworthy sons are heard of but never a mother.
You show compassion and shower nectar on all
and remove the miseries of the miserable
O' mother dark and invincible...

We do not ask for money, wealth nor silver nor gold
O' mother we ask for a small corner in your heart,
You set aside every one's discord and
        save them from shame
You look after the honour of all chaste women
O' Mother dark and invincible...

Sri Hanuman ji ki Arti

Arti kije Hanuman lala ki,
Dusht dalan Raghunath kala ki,
Jake bal se girwar kaanpe
Bhoot peshaach nikat nahin jhanke
Lanka so kot samundr se khaaee
Jaat pawan sut baar na laayee,
Dey beesha Rahgunath pathaye
Lankapraja valli Siya sudh laye
Jagmug jyoti Avadhpur raja
Ghanta tall pakhawaj baaja
Shakti baan lagaa Laxman ko
Laaye sanjeevan Laxman jiyayo
Paith pataal tori yum kaare
Aniravan ki bhuja ukharey
Arti kijay jaisee taisee
Dhruv Prahlad, Vibhishan jaisee
Sur nar munni arti utarain
Jai jai Kapiraj ubaren
Baaren bhuja say asur sanhaaray
Dahini bhuja sur sant ubaray
Lank prajavalli asur sanhaaray
Raja Ram ke kaaj sanvaray
Anjani putra maha baldayak
Dev sant ke sada sahayak
Vidhvans lank kiya Raghurai Tulsidas kapi arti gaayee
Jo Hanumanji ki arti gaave, Basee Baikunt bahar naheen
     aavey

Sri Hanuman ji ki Arti

Let us perform the arti of Hanuman, the beloved
   the destroyer of the wicked and a part of Ram
His power makes the mountains shiver and shake
Ghost and goblin cannot come near
The Fort of Lanka and the moat around it
   was crossed by the son of the wind in one stride
He did not have to try again and again
Sri Raghunath made Him promise to go with a mission
   and return with success
After burning Lanka he brought the tidings of Sita
And Ram, the king of Avadh shone like a glittering light
There was the sound of drums and the rythem of Pakhawaj
   (a kind of long drum)
When Laxman was hit by the arrow of 'Power'
   he brought the 'Sanjeevni' and brought back Laxman
   to life
Going to 'Patal lok' he broke the prison of Yama
   and broke the arm of Ahirvan
Do the arti like was done by
   Dhruv, Prahlad and Vibhishan
Gods, men and saints perform his arti
   singing the victory of the King of the monkeys
He killed the demons with his left arm
   and saved the saints with his right arm
He burnt Lanka and killed the demons
And completed with success the mission of Ram
The son of Anjani, of great valour and strength
He always looks after the Devtas and saints
When Ram destroyed Lanka everyone sang
'Your Arti' — so says Tulsidas
He, whoever, sings the arti of Hanumanji
Will always live in the abode of Vishnu (Vaikunth)
   and will never be born again.

Index